ABODE OF FAIRIES

ABODE OF FAIRIES

Lucknow's Parikhana

PC Sarkar

KALPAZ

ISBN: 978-93-5324-943-4 (HB)

First Published, 2022

Published by

Kalpaz Publications
C-30, Satyawati Nagar,
Delhi – 110052
Ph.: 011-47034999, 9811692060
www.kalpazpublications.com
E-mail: kalpaz@hotmail.com

Printed at: Gyan Press, Delhi.

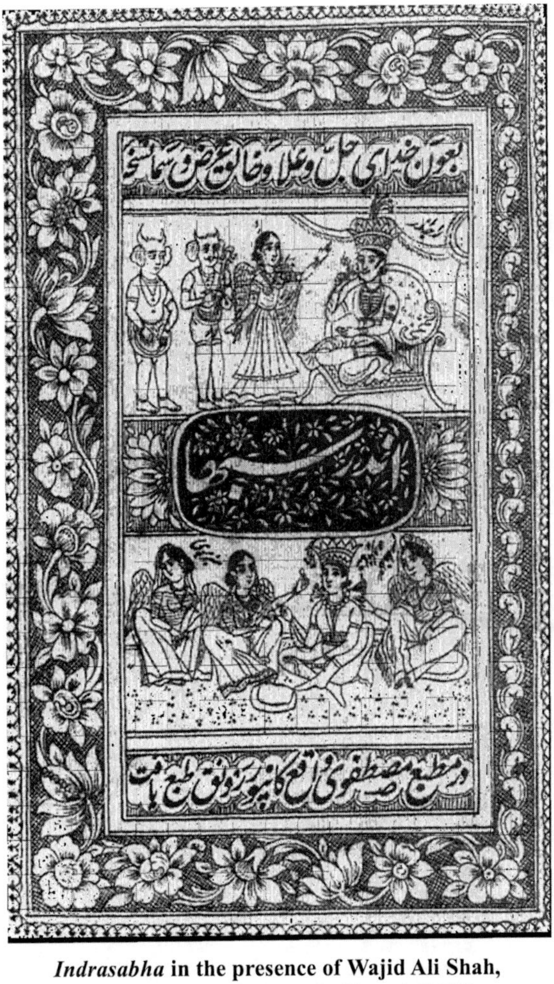

Indrasabha **in the presence of Wajid Ali Shah,**
by Agha Hasan Amanat Lakhnavi (1853)

This book is dedicated to the people of Lucknow
and to their Last King,
Jān-é-Alam Wajid Ali Shah "Akhtar"

- PC Sarkar

Contents

उल्फत ने तेरी हम को तो रखा न कहीं का
दरया का न जंगल का समां का न ज़मीन का

इक़लीम-ए-मानी में अमल हो गया मेरा
दुनिया में भरोसा था किसे ताज-ओ नगीन का

तक़दीर ने क्या क़ुतुब-ए-फलक मुझ को बनाया
मोहताज मेरा पाँव रहा ख़ाना-ए-ज़ीं का

एक बोरिये के तख़्त पे औक़ात बसर की
ज़ाहिद भी मुक़ल्लिद रहा सज्जदा नशीन का

"अख़्तर" क़लम-ए-फ़िक्र के भी अश्क है जारी
क्या हाल लिखूं अपने दिल-ए-ज़ार ओ हाज़िन का

– वाजिद अली शाह "अख़्तर"

My love for you has left me nowhere
Neither of the river, nor forest, neither of the heavens
nor of earth

I remained occupied in realm of meanings
Who in this world had faith in the crown and gems

My fate made me the axis of the sky
My feet remained tied in the house of saddles

My status was that of one on a throne made of mat
A recluse, a disciple of one who is a caretaker of tombs

"Akhtar" even the pen of thought is in tears
What to write on the condition of my melancholic heart

– Wajid Ali Shah "Akhtar"

Exordium

1

Prologue

Wajid Ali Shah, the eleventh and last ruler of Awadh, was born on July 30, 1822. He was the second son of Amjad Ali Shah and Mallika Kishwar, the former respectfully addressed as *Hazrat* and the latter popularly known as *Janab-e-Alia* (Lucknow's famous market, *Hazratganj* is named in honour of Amjad Ali Shah "Hazrat"). Wajid Ali would later hold the honorific titles of *Abul Mansoor Nasir-ud-Din Badshah-e-Adil Kaiser-e-Zaman Arangha Sultan-e-Alam Mohammad Wajid Ali Shah Bahadur*. But he would remain popular in history as Nawab Wajid Ali Shah, although he was never a Nawab. During his birth, he was not in the line of succession for the throne of Awadh; he was merely the nephew of the then ruling (first) king (*Badshah*) of Awadh, Ghazi-ud-Din Haider. His elder half-brother was Mirza Mohammad Mustafa Ali (born in 1819); he had a younger brother, Sikander Hashmat (born in 1828) and a sister, Ashraf un-Nisan (born in 1834), as well as other foster siblings. It is said that after his birth, astrologers had expressed a poor view of his fortunes, as a result of which, he dressed in saffron on his birthdays (an offshoot of Hindu rites and rituals, including the observance of *chatti*, the sixth day of the birth of a child. This is of no surprise, considering the composite culture of Awadh in those days).

Wajid Ali Shah's childhood remained unspectacular, without any special rights or privileges. This was due to the fact that he was at best an ordinary prince or *mushirzada*, and not a *shahzada* or royal prince. Like other youngsters in the household, he was given lessons in *Farsi* (Persian) language as well as trained in outdoor activities suited for a nobleman's son. Syed Imdad Hussain Khan was appointed as his private tutor or *ataleeq*. (The same Imdad Hussain would be conferred the title of Amin-ud-Daula and elevated to the post of *Wazir* during the reign of Amjad Ali Shah, father of Wajid Ali Shah). Like Amjad Ali Shah, Imdad too was a devout Muslim, for whom music and dance were *haram* (forbidden under Islamic law). It is not clear where and how young Wajid Ali imbibed his keen sense and interest for the performing arts, as well as for literature and poetry. There is an interesting anecdote, about the young *mushirzada,* who apparently had a habit of keeping time with his feet during lessons. For this, he had his ears boxed by his *ataleeq*, which resulted in the prince becoming partially deaf.

1837 was a landmark year for the young Wajid Ali. His parents had contemplated on his marriage, but due to various reasons, the early marriage proposals could not materialise. Eventually, during the reign of Nasir-ud-Din Haider (second king of Awadh), Wajid Ali's first marriage was solemnised in 1837 at *Shah Manzil*, Lucknow, to Mallika Muqqadara-i-Azma, popularly known as *Alam Ara Begum*. Her parents were Nawab Sayyid Ali Khan Bahadur and Barati Khanum (Nawab Dulhan Begum), the latter being a daughter of James Zulfiqar Martin, an adopted son of Major General Claude Martin. Nawab Ali Khan was the cousin of Ali Naqi Khan, who later became the *Wazir* (=Prime Minister) in the court of Wajid Ali. At the time of her marriage, Alam Ara was reportedly about twenty years of age, and Wajid Ali was merely fifteen years old. The night of July 7, 1837 saw the untimely death of Nasir-ud-Din Haider, the second king of Awadh. A discussion on the conspiracy theories behind his untimely death is beyond the scope of this book. However, it is generally believed that he was poisoned to death at the instigation of the British and as a result of palace intrigues within his own court. Nevertheless, with the installation of Nasir-ud-Daula as third king of Awadh, young

Wajid Ali came into the direct line of succession for the throne of Awadh.

Nasir-ud-Daula was around sixty three years of age at the time of his coronation by the British. He was the third son of Sa'adat Ali Khan, the sixth Nawab of Awadh. By a quirk of faith, he succeeded his nephew, Nasir-ud-Din Haider. During the chaos that ensued during his coronation, with Badshah Begum (dowager Queen of Ghazi-ud-Din Haider) rallying forth for the candidature of Munna Jaan (Faridun Bakht) for the throne and the British stoutly resisting the move, this venerable old man, together with his family consisting of his eldest son, Amjad Ali Shah, grandson Wajid Ali Shah and few others were subjected to severe intimidation by the supporters of Badshah Begum. However, the British managed to have their way, and Nasir-ud-Daula was installed as king of Awadh. He ruled for five years (1837- 42) as Mohammad Ali Shah Bahadur, and was succeeded by Amjad Ali Shah, son of his second queen, Jahanara Begum (Khetu Begum) in 1842. During the reign of Mohammad Ali Shah, the unfortunate Wajid Ali had to be satisfied with a meagre monthly allowance. His father, then *Wali Ahad* (crown prince), granted Wajid Ali a monthly allowance of Rs 500 and Rs 400 for his wife. With the coronation of Amjad Ali Shah, Wajid Ali Shah became the heir designate or *Wali Ahad*. As part of his training in administration, young Wajid also served as *peshkar* to his father. All these related and un-related events paved the way for Wajid Ali Shah to ultimately become the king of Awadh after the death of his father, Amjad Ali Shah, in 1847. In fact, Mustafa Ali, the eldest son of Amjad Ali Shah, had been earlier repudiated by his father in 1838, deprived of his titles and even imprisoned, with no hope of becoming the claimant to the throne. (Four decades later, his titles would be restored by the British, but this would be too little and too late). The reason behind Mustafa Ali's conflict with Amjad Ali Shah appears to have been his propensity to complain to the king (his grandfather), against his own father, about day-to-day events in the court. Historians have also surmised that

Mustafa was *persona non grata* for another reason: he was not the son of *Khas Mahal*, Mallika Kishwar. But this is open to question.

Superficially, it appeared that the British had wanted to depose Wajid Ali due to his "misrule", thereby saving the kingdom of Awadh from any catastrophe (although the main intention had been to gobble up Awadh anyhow). Outram had tried to pour oil on troubled waters by approaching *Janab-e-Alia* Mallika Kishwar, who had not only refused to bow down before the unjustified and unreasonable demands of the Resident; she had proposed that Sikander Hashmat, the king's younger brother to take over, at best, rather than lose the kingdom altogether. This, of course, was unacceptable to the British. Apparently, Mustafa's candidature for the *masnad* had also been proposed by his grandmother Muqqadara Azma, widow of Mohammad Ali Shah (discussed later).

To come back to the travails of young Wajid Ali, the prince too did not forget the box on his ears by his *ataleeq*; the latter had become *Wazir* under his father, the king. One of the early actions of Wajid Ali after his own ascension to the Awadh royal seat or *masnad*, was to replace Amin-ud-Daula with Ali Naqi Khan as *Wazir*.

Even as a prince and heir designate, Wajid Ali had given full vent to his creative talents in the performing arts. A "house" later known as *Rashq-e-Iram*, was set aside for training nubile young women in song and dance. This house would later metamorphose into the full fledged *Parikhana* in the *Kaiserbagh* palace complex. This was despite the fact that he was already married to Alam Ara Begum, who was an accomplished poetess, using her first name, *Alam* in her *ghazals* and *masnavis*; similarly Wajid Ali composed under the pen name (*takhallus*) of *Akhtar* or Akhtar *Pia*. With time, Wajid Ali preferred to be addressed as *Jané Alam* or *Jān-é-Álam* and the two spent many happy moments together in the initial stages of their married life. Sadly, due to Wajid Ali's amorous ways, as more and more women of all shades and hues entered the young prince's life, the royal marriage gradually collapsed and Alam Ara Begum's importance in the Awadh court decreased with time.

Saddled with a strained relationship with her mother-in-law, Mallika Kishwar, the role of Begum Alam Ara was effectively finished in the royal court, even though she would be the mother (*Khas Mahal*) of the crown prince of the Awadh throne. This was in complete contrast to the respect and awe that Mallika Kishwar, the Queen Mother, herself commanded in the Awadh court.

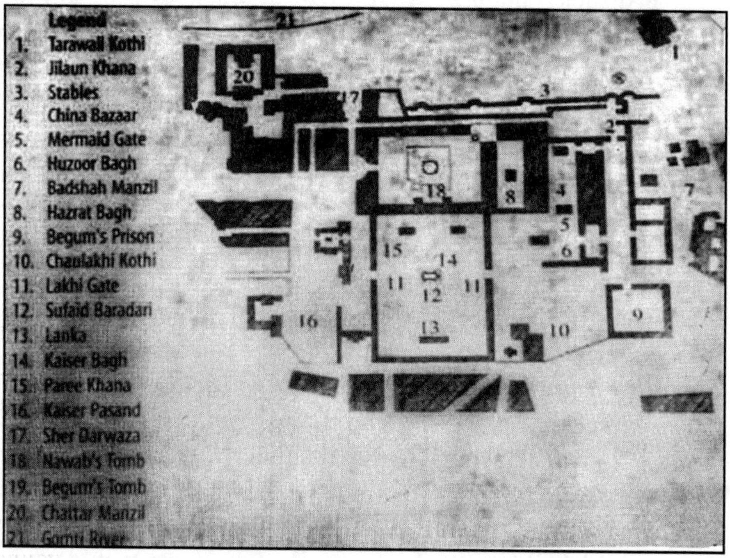

Fig. 1 : Layout of *Kaiserbagh* in 1857, Unidentified Source.

By his own admission, Wajid Ali "excelled in making new discoveries and constructing new buildings (*Shahanshah Manzil*, a winter palace; *Makan-e-Khas*, the summer palace and *Falak Sair* for the monsoon season)." He created a royal pleasure garden called *Huzur (Huzoor) Bagh*, the first hand description of which can be read later in this book. The young prince was a teetotaller (which he remained throughout his life), a devout *Shi'a* Muslim, and immensely respectful towards his parents. However, his relations with his first wife remained rocky throughout his lifetime. Wajid Ali was merely twenty five years of age when he had ascended the throne. The seeds of his amorous and creative talents as well as artistic sensitivities had been laid out well before his ascension. The fledgling *Parikhana* was also functional, albeit in a house designated for the purpose and not in a dedicated building complex which would later be built within the *Kaiserbagh* palace complex.

Parikhana - Myth and Mythos

To dispel a popular urban myth of Lucknow, the present building in *Kaiserbagh* designated as *Parikhana* is *not* the original *Parikhana*. The Foundation Stone of Canning College (present day Bhatkhande Music Institute), Lucknow had been laid on November 13, 1867 (Sarkar, 2021). The construction was completed in 1879, after several delays. This building was built on the *grounds* of the erstwhile *Parikhana* proper, which had been demolished post 1857, but the exact date of demolition is not known. According to a paper read at the Royal Institute of British Architects, by the Executive Engineer, JA Willmore, "*the soil on which the building was erected was found to consist of 2 feet of rubbish, remains of former old buildings and below that, of sand.*" The architectural plans and elevations of the Canning College building (now housing the Bhatkhande Music Institute) are available on record (Brandreth, 1879). Therefore, to state that the present day Bhatkhande Music Institute is actually housed in the Nawabi building of the erstwhile *Parikhana* would be an outright falsehood. Together with several other buildings of *Kaiserbagh* palace complex, *Parikhana* too had been demolished during the period 1858 - 1867.

So what was the building of *Parikhana* actually like? Photographs of the area by several people unequivocally indicate that the central quadrangle of *Kaiserbagh* was lined with a range of double-storeyed buildings, with colonnaded verandas. The *Parikhana* was the northernmost building, parallel to the tombs of Sa'adat Ali Khan and Khurshid Zadi. Unlike other buildings, it did not have a colonnaded veranda on the first floor. Instead it had small terraces, each having a low balcony. Each individual terrace had three arched doorways leading inside. It can be concluded

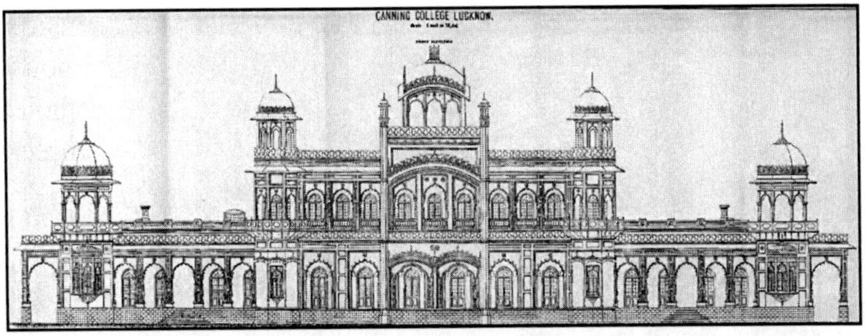

Fig. 2: Front Elevation of Canning College building.

that the individual terraces lead to individual apartments, where the *paris* resided. The roofline had a perforated arcade, similar to other Nawabi buildings. Like other *Kaiserbagh* buildings, *Parikhana* too was heavily stuccoed, with the usual pediments and oriel windows. The centre of the building had a substantial portico, surmounted by the usual arched, decorative element seen in other Nawabi buildings, e.g. gateway of *Sibtainabad Imambara*. The portico was flush opposite an elevated marble pavilion (vaguely in the usual square canopy Nawabi style), resembling a small *baradari*, which is not extant, and a marble bridge, which can be seen even today. From atop the *Roshan-ud-Daula Kothi*, Beato had photographed the building's southern facade in 1858, together with other buildings of *Kaiserbagh*. It indicated that *Parikhana* too had been considerably damaged in the bombardment. That some buildings of *Kaiserbagh* had been restored by the British was evident from few wide-angle photographs of *Parikhana* and its environs from 1863. Fresh landscaping of the area had also been carried out. John Edward Sache had photographed *Kaiserbagh* (including a restored *Parikhana*) in 1865. Thus, it is not clear as to how and why it was subsequently razed to the ground to make way for Canning College in 1867, within a period of approximately two years.

None of the *Kaiserbagh* buildings of the central quadrangle had central courtyards; in fact, they were equipped with backyards. But *Parikhana* seemed to be an exception. Sache's photograph,

Fig. 3: *Parikhana*, with tombs of Sa'adat Ali Khan and Khurshid Zadi, in the background (1863).

Fig. 4: *Parikhana*, with tombs of Sa'adat Ali Khan and Khurshid Zadi, in the background (1863).

Fig. 5: Vintage view of *Parikhana* facing marble bridge and pavilion.

Fig. 6: Vintage view of Canning College building, now facing marble bridge.

possibly taken from the tomb of Sa'adat Ali Khan, reveals that the structure had at least four interconnected courtyards (albeit not very large ones). Hence it was a true *zenana* structure, ensuring privacy for its occupants. There is no known photograph or image of the northern facade of *Parikhana*; it's entrance was obviously from the south side *via* the portico described above.

Fig. 7: *Paris* in *Kaiserbagh*, Unidentified Artist.

It has often been conjectured by different writers that *Parikhana* was a heavily guarded establishment, the guards being of African descent (possibly Abyssinian). Wajid Ali's narrative does not support this claim. He frequently mentioned a female guard (*daroga*) Najm un-Nisa Begum, with whom he shared a close relationship (not sexual). She was certainly not of African origin. In fact, she was around forty five years old, and an aunt of Alam Ara Begum, as also related to Ali Naqi Khan, the *Wazir*. Another *daroga* mentioned in the text was Mir Mohammad Mehdi. There is no mention of any woman of African origin on security detail.

After the untimely demise of Najm un-Nisa, her charge was given to an Umrao Begum, on the recommendation of *daroga* Mohammad Hussain Ali Khan, who held the title of Mohammad Moat-mud Ali Khan. A Nishat-ud-Daula was the *daroga* in charge of singers and dancers. A *daroga* of the *zenana* was Mohammad Sharif Ali Khan. But the *zenana* was a different entity from the *Parikhana*. The king did mention *paris* like Shirin, Laila, Fiza and Ambar, who were of African descent. But none of them were on guard detail; they were mere attendants. That the king had sexual relations with at least one (if not all) of them is indicated by the fact that Fiza's daughter, Jahanara Begum, was an offspring of the king himself. Unfortunately she passed away at the tender age of three years, which seems to have devastated the ruler. However, in *Ishqnama*, Wajid Ali did mention *Turkish* female guards, who prevented unauthorised entry of strangers into the initial *Parikhana.* As *Wali Ahad,* the prince had "*reserved a small house for educating paris in music and song. It was decorated with a lot of thought and became a Parikhana – a challenge for the heavens themselves. White marble flooring was laid, which was decorated with beautiful porcelain vases. Expensive cots and beds were arranged in profusion. The entrance was guarded by Turkish female guards, who prevented unauthorised entry of strangers.*" However, after his coronation and the building of the formal *Parikhana* within the *Kaiserbagh* palace complex, there is no known description of either the exterior or the interior of this dedicated building. For all practical purposes, the musical soirees were held in open air; *Parikhana* was actually a finishing school for women, training them in music and dance. It also provided them accommodation. For cultural events, *Kaiserbagh* was replete with marble pavilions of various capacities; it also had the massive *Lanka*, an open air auditorium. The present Amir-ud-Daula Library stands on the grounds of the erstwhile *Lanka*. The *Rahas Manzil* was notable for the performance of *rahas* within its premises (discussed elsewhere). Also, to state that the British built the Marris College of Music in the premises of *Parikhana* is an outright falsehood. After Canning College shifted to its new premises in *Badshah Bagh*, its former building in *Kaiserbagh* was to house the Provincial Museum. The Marris College of Music was established in the premises in 1926 - the institution being formally inaugurated by the then Governor of United Provinces, Sir William Sinclair Marris. This music college later metamorphosed into the Bhatkhande Music Institute in 1966.

Ishqnama **a.k.a.** ***Parikhana*** **(The Book)**

Aloys Sprenger was an Austrian scholar with a medical degree, who had joined the British East India Company's medical service in order to pursue in India, his real passion, *i.e.* the study of oriental literature. Soon after the coronation of Wajid Ali in February, 1847, Fort William appointed Sprenger as an extra Assistant to the British Resident at Lucknow, in December 1847, with the sole objective of cataloguing the extensive collection of works in Arabic and Persian literature in the libraries of the king at Lucknow. This massive collection had not been built by Wajid Ali single-handedly; it was a legacy of the former Nawabs and rulers of Awadh, (especially Ghazi-ud-Din Haider), which seemed to have become so voluminous that it could not be housed in a single location and was also not catalogued and stored properly.

According to Sprenger (1854), the Royal Library had been initially housed in the *Daulat Khana* palace complex. Later, it was split up into three sections. The "valuable literary works", more than three thousand in number, were preserved in a garden house of *Moti Mahal* palace and the "elegant books" were stored in the *Farhat Baksh* palace, where the king resided (the *Kaiserbagh* palace was not yet ready then). The third lot was housed in the first floor of the *Tope Khana* or arsenal, in a pitiable condition, many destroyed by rats and termites.

During the storming of *Kaiserbagh* in 1858, and subsequent ransacking of the palace complex by British troops and Sikh soldiers, a lavish volume bound in leather, gilded and silvered had been confiscated, among other treasures and valuables. Inscribed *Nazm-e-Ishqnama Hind-ba-Taswirat* in *Farsi*, it eventually ended up in the custody of John Lawrence, who later presented it to Queen Victoria in 1859. The book remained as a curiosity in the Royal Library of Windsor Castle and was known more for its depiction of the customs of the Nawabi court of Lucknow, instead of being a firsthand narrative of deposed king Wajid Ali Shah's early life and romantic predilections, which it actually was. The volume contained exquisitely painted illustrations with the text therein written in large *nastaliq* (calligraphic style, with clear, easy to read hand-writing) script. Semi-autobiographical in nature, it covered intimate details and erotic encounters of Wajid Ali Shah as a crown prince, details of the death of his father, Amjad Ali Shah, and the subsequent coronation of young Wajid Ali himself. Together with detailed descriptions of the dancing girls or *paris*, their induction, conduct, training, romantic trysts and frequent indiscretions, the book also had scattered references to the day-to-day life of the young prince / ruler, his vanity, his extreme respect and regard for his parents, his own creative talents in dance, music and drama

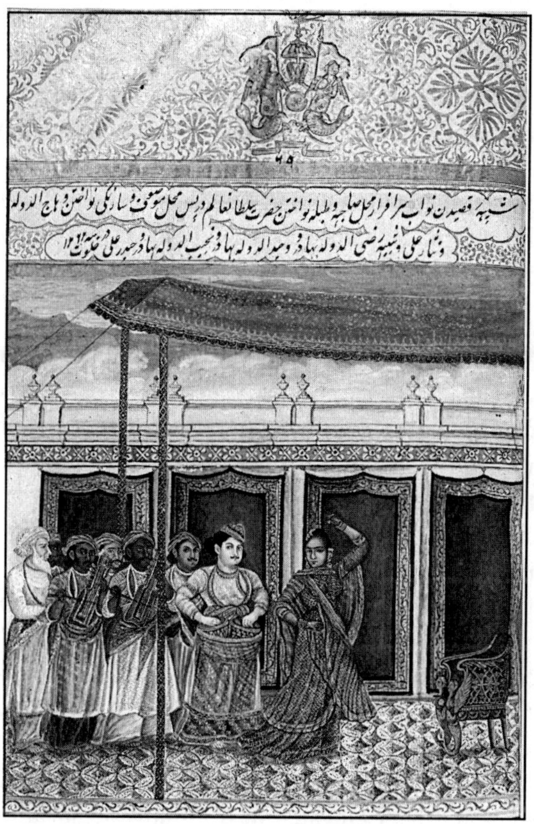

Fig. 8: Safaraz Pari dances while Wajid Ali plays percussion, *Ishqnama.*

(and garden architecture!), as well as detailed depictions of the cultural events that he had organised and attended from time to time. The account was chronological, verisimilar, some-times tragic, occasionally hilarious, highly romanticised, and at times monotonous. The text was often dramatised and embellished by hyperbole. A common thread of eroticism bound the entire piece of writing together. Written over a period of two years, this semi-autobiographical manuscript had been completed in 1849 by the young king, at the age of twenty six.

Was there a demarcation in *Parikhana*, based on caste and / or community of the women themselves? The actual narrative in the book has such no details, although Sharar (1989) had mentioned that the courtesans were divided into three groups. The first group were professional prostitutes, belonging to the *Kanchan* tribes of Punjab and Delhi. The second group comprised of the *Chunawalis*, whose primary occupation was to sell *chunam* (lime mortar). The third group originally belonged to Gujarat, and were known as *Nagarnt*.

It may be noted that Wajid Ali's autobiographical details, although hedonistic and narcissistic, were totally devoid of any pangs of conscience or feelings of contrition on part of the author. The prince / young king was aware of his royal status, religious beliefs, musical talents, good looks and sexual charms; he went about his ways without a shred of regret or remorse. In the book, he appeared in all the paintings except three - with a halo, as a prince and wearing a spiked haloed crown, as a king. The women were almost always depicted in dancing postures, but possessing unsmiling, surly looks. *Ishqnama / Parikhana* was replete with references to a Sarfaraz Begum, with whom the young king was apparently besotted with. Sarfaraz was a married woman, around twenty seven years of age, with a pock-marked face. She had entered Wajid Ali Shah's establishment as a *pari*, after divorcing her husband, and later elevated to the status of Sarfaraz Mahal. This particular lady in question seems to have caused much heartburn and anguish to the young king, due to her erratic and unfaithful ways. She appeared in ten of the paintings but was later divorced by the king and left to fend for herself. In Folio 238 of *Ishqnama*, Sarfaraz was depicted as a dancer, with the king having left his royal seat and playing the *tabla* as accompaniment (while standing, the instrument apparently hanging from his chest) - a truly unusual and uncommon depiction. The *tabla* is never played from a standing position in this manner - at best it can be kept on an elevated surface, like a stand or table with the player then playing from an upright position. This atypical depiction reminds one of Sleeman's derogatory comment about "*the king's* (Wajid Ali Shah) *ambition seems to be limited to the reputation of being the best drum-beater, dancer, and poet of the day. He is utterly unfit to reign.*"

In a recent paper (Singh, 2021), there are interesting interpretations of Wajid Ali's exhibitionist conduct; firstly, there is a comparison with Nasir-al-Din Shah Qajar, a contemporary Persian ruler, who had ruled between 1848-1896 and had documented his harem by photographing the women. Secondly, there is this angle of moral "right" and sexuality of a ruler, within the culturally complex, socio-political milieu, royal aspirations, tastes, influences, and underlying traditions of erstwhile Awadh, as narrated by Waqar Tabrizi, a Persian traveller at Lucknow. The reader is left wondering as to whether the actions and inactions of the prince / young king as described in *Ishqnama* (with accompanying artwork) were simply youthful transgressions or the "visual culture" actually played a prominent role in maintaining and fortifying the power of the ruler in mid-nineteenth century Awadh - then a site of socio-political negotiation and contestation between two major contenders: Wajid Ali Shah and the British East India Company.

Another interesting theory on the genesis of *Ishqnama* (Pandey, 2013), brings forth the premise that Wajid Ali had been exposed to child abuse and the follies of youth, coupled with pressures of the court. And that he had become weary of it all. The semi-autobiographical account was simply a sort of catharsis, for his pent-up emotions and frustrations as a young man. This theory gains credence from the young ruler's own declaration about his agonizing past and betrayals that he had faced. *Ishqnama* had concluded abruptly on a dark, brooding note, detailing the perfidy of his female companions, the fickleness of the female sex, the death of his young children, coupled with his own painful illness.

Fig. 9: Wajid Ali receives Mehak Pari a.k.a. Hazrat Mahal, *Ishqnama.*

One of the Folios depicted Wajid Ali Shah receiving Iftikhar un-Nisa, later Begum Hazrat Mahal, famous for her role in the events of 1857. The lady, with a proud visage, stands alone before the king, but she is no beauty. Born Muhammadi Khanum, she was the daughter of Mir Ghulam Hussain of Faizabad; she was also called Mehak Pari; this earned her the unfortunate sobriquet of 'Nautch Girl' from the British (the Rani of Jhansi was similarly called 'Jezebel' by them). As subsequent history would show, this nautch girl would be more than a match for the might of the East India Company in the events of 1857 – 58. Even after she had been defeated, she refused to surrender and preferred to remain in exile in Nepal. Her brusque and terse rejoinder to Queen Victoria's Proclamation dated November 1, 1858 would be more than enough to earn her a place in history.

Despite the fact that this particular book, possibly the original version of *Ishqnama* had been left behind in *Kaiserbagh,* it is wholly plausible that the king had carried a copy (or versions thereof) to Calcutta. This is because lithographic copies and Urdu translations of his works became available later on, including translations of the *Ishqnama* - the latter being called *Mahal Khana Shahi* or *Tarikh-e-Pari Khana* (Mirza Fida Ali) and *Parikhana* (Tehsin Khan Sarwari). Earlier, the deposed king had installed a printing press, *Matbá-i-Sultani* in *Metia Burz*, from where several of his latter literary compositions (many in Urdu) like *Nājo* (1868), *Dulhan* (1873) and *Banî* (1877) were published. The initial Urdu version of *Ishqnama* was also printed from this very printing press, the translator being Wajid Ali himself, who gave it a *masnavi* form with rhyming couplets. The *Ishqnama* also acquired an English title: *Customs of the Court of Oudh*, due to reasons elaborated above. *Mahal Khana Shahi* had been produced by famous poet of yesteryears, Khanjar Lakhnavi (1914). The poet's name was actually Mirza Fida Ali, and it was purported that he had obtained an authentic copy of *Parikhana* from the personal library of Yusuf Hussain Saheb, a barrister-at-law. The *Parikhana* was later printed in *Devanagari* script (Iqbal Bahadur, 1982; Shakeel Siddique, 2017). The original book was in the form of *dastaans* (tales or stories with detailed, often unnecessary descriptions). The authors of the *Parikhana* and *Mahal Khana Shahi or Mahal-e-Shahi Khana* seemed to have transformed *Ishqnama*'s poetry and images into a simplified prose. Some of the *dastaans* were reportedly removed in later versions, possibly because they did not reflect well on the king. That the king could be sensitive in such matters is amply indicated in an incident regarding *Taaron Wali Kothi*, the observatory built in Lucknow earlier during the reign of Nasir-ud-Din Haider. The king had ordered the closure of the observatory, simply because Sayyed Kamal-ud-Din Haider, a translator employed in the observatory, had shown him in poor light in his book titled *Sawanih-Hayat-Salatin Awadh Vol. II,* also known as *Qaysar-al-Twarikh*; the annoyed king had also apparently tried to gift some costly apparatus of the defunct observatory to one of his *begums*, a move which had been resisted by the British. But we are digressing.

Although originally named *Ishqnama* (Book of Love / Chronicle of Love), the term *Parikhana* was consistently used in the text, while referring to the training school established by Wajid Ali Shah. Hence it is but obvious that the title: *Parikhana*, should become more popular for the book itself in due course of time. It is generally accepted that the book had 3 chapters and 126 narrations. Despite the fact that Wajid Ali's memoir was replete with hyperbole, it is not that he had been untruthful. Rajab Ali Beg Surur, a courtier of the king and a famous writer of prose, recalled in his book *Fasāna-e-Ibrat*, the following details:

"Hundreds of attendants had learned their duties through a great deal of instruction. There were uproarious jalsas of great pomp, going from morning till evening. The dance, from the very first beat of the unique tals, included every (gesture of) intoxicated playfulness; the songs were of a new style. The instruments were unique, costing hundreds of thousands of rupees. (All) things that were there were extraordinary and superior. According to the

saying, "Everyone says this, (only) God's name is better than that." Time after time, fortune favoured men and women. Another jalsa was prepared, that was better than this, this was better than that, a treat of extraordinary taste was shared (Castro, 2016)."

Was young Wajid Ali inspired by autobiographical works of the great Mughals like *Baburnama* (which provided an insight into the literary, intellectual, and cultural world of Babur), the founder of the Mughal empire, or the *Tuzk-e-Jahangiri / Jahangirnama*, which followed the tradition of Jahangir's great grandfather? But these were accounts of entire lifetimes of the respective rulers. *Ishqnama* was completed in 1849 when Wajid Ali was merely twenty six years of age, covering the life and times of the young prince, from when he was a young boy, eight years old, his youth as *Wali Ahad* and then as a young king for two years. It described the agonies and the ecstasies of a youth, who lived a carefree life, and then had the responsibility of ruling a prosperous kingdom thrust upon him. While one may look at disdain at the intimate descriptions provided in the book, it must be remembered that administrative responsibilities and British rapaciousness were also preying upon the mind of the young prince / king. The former had already expressed that, *"The kingdom of Oudh was a cherry which would one day drop into their mouths.*" It is perhaps an irony of fate that an original copy of the *Ishqnama* too should fall like a cherry in the mouths of British marauders, when they ransacked *Kaiserbagh* in 1858.

Taking into account the various versions and *avatars* of the book (as on date, there is no known English version of the book, *Parikhana* or its numerous *avatars*), the narrative could be broadly divisible into the following:

(a) Sexual exploitation and escapades during childhood (b) Relations with various women and their induction into the training school, followed by harem (c) Description of first marriage (*nikah*) (d) Few details of children and their births (e) Establishment of the training school, *Parikhana* (f) Appointment of maestros as instructors and performers in the field of dance, instrumental and vocal music (g) Description of various cultural events and musical soirees (h) Conflict of various *begums,* among themselves and with the ruler (i) Agony and ecstasies of love (j) Various efforts of the *paris* and begums to prove their fidelity to the ruler (k) Ailments (mental and physical) of the ruler (l) Infidelity and inconsistency of some *paris* and *begums* (m) Scepticism on the faithfulness of the courtiers and means thereof to clear the doubts (n) Interactions with his father, the king; subsequent coronation of the prince (o) Disappointment and frustration with the female sex, with particular reference to the *paris* and *mut'ah* wives (p) The end of *Parikhana.*

Although the live activities of the *Parikhana* seemed to have ceased during Wajid Ali Shah's rule itself, even before his deposition, once at Calcutta, his musical talents blossomed forth once again, especially after his release in July 1859, from house arrest at Fort William. *Jalsakhana* in *Metia Burz* would then become the latter-day *avatar* of the defunct *Parikhana* of Lucknow. By 1877, there were 22 *jalsa*s (assemblies) receiving musical training in *Metia Burz*. These included 4 *raqqas* (dance instructors), the *jalsa* female performers being trained by 15 *kalawants* (professional music teachers, well versed in the pedagogy of music), one *khemta* (Bengali dance form) instructor, 2 *pakhawaj* (two headed percussion drum) players, 23 *tabla* (a pair of twin hand drums) players, 46 *sarangi* (a stringed instrument, played with a bow) players, 22 *manjira* (cymbal) players, 2 *dholak* (a two-headed hand drum, a folk percussion instrument) players, one *sursingar* (stringed instrument, resembling the *sarod*) player, a 19-person *naqqara* or *nagada* (large drum with a rounded back and a hide head, usually played in pairs) ensemble, together with 6 *mehfil* (concert) attendants (Williams, 2014). The show was to go on.

The *Paris* For Real

In 1874, Daroga Abbas Ali had published a volume called *The Beauties of Lucknow* in English and *Hasina-e-Lakhnau* in Urdu, "consisting of twenty four selected photographed portraits of the most celebrated and popular living histrionic singers, dancing girls, and actresses of the Oudh Court and of Lucknow." Abbas Ali had also produced similar albums, containing photographs, together with short write-ups of old Lucknow buildings called *The Lucknow Album, Containing a Series of Fifty Photographic Views of Lucknow And Its Environs* (1874) and of the rajas and ta'aluqdars of Awadh titled *An Illustrated Historical Album of The Rajas and Taaluqdars of Oudh* (1880). This does not necessarily mean that his photographs were of the same period; it merely indicated their dates of compilation and publication. In fact, he had been active before and after the events of 1857, although, being a government municipal engineer, his sympathies apparently lay with the British.

Fig. 10: Umrao Jaan, holding fan with Awadh royal insignia.

Records of the *Beauties* Album are available with the Alkazi Collection, George Eastman Museum, New York Public Library Digital Collections and few private owners, although in some cases, the names (and spellings) and captions do not match. While any number of motives and intentions can be attributed to the author (Patel, 2015; Hansen, 2020), a brief analysis of the Album would not be out of place here. For example, all twenty four photographs (*Annexure II*) mention "Dancing Girl Oudh Court of Lucknow." It is well known that there was no Oudh Court in 1874. One of the dancers, Umrao Jaan (Plate 11) is actually holding a fan which sports the royal twin fish (mermaid symbol of Wajid Ali Shah, to be more specific) insignia of Awadh. Two of the dancers, Lal Pari, Plate 16 and Pukhraj Pari, Plate 17 sport fake wings like fairies

Fig. 11: Pukhraj Pari sporting fake wings.

(*paris*). The term *Indur Subha* (*Indrasabha*) is used in four plates (Plates 16 - 19). Wajid Ali's fascination for Lord Indra's court of celestial dancers is discussed in later chapters of this book.

Without going into semantics, it seems safe to assume that these ladies actually belonged to the *Parikhana* of Wajid Ali Shah, although they may have been dispossessed later, with the winding up of the *Parikhana* establishment and the events of 1857. That many of the *paris* had absolutely no compunction about appearing in public (which rankled Wajid Ali), it would be no great surprise for the reader that they agreed to pose before the camera of Abbas Ali at some point of time. And the photographer / engineer managed to get the collection published after he had retired from active service, because the work had been adulatory for the Nawabi era in an oblique manner.

Another alternative narrative could be that Abbas Ali staged an elaborate pantomime - collecting girls (not necessarily dancers), providing them with appropriate costumes and paraphernalia, photographing them and providing fake captions. But the latter theory (as proposed by some writers) seems to be highly improbable and pointless.

2

Connoisseur and Maestro

It has already been mentioned earlier that Wajid Ali had an inherent leaning and affinity towards song and dance since his childhood. In fact, he understood and accepted the fact that feminine beauty and accompanying music could, at times, even overpower him and influence his better judgement. Therefore, occasionally he deliberately chose to stay away from musical soirees, simply to gather his wits about him. The description of his own encounter with Waziran, a professional courtesan, in the early pages of *Ishqnama* as, "*I could no longer eat, drink or sleep properly. Her eyes so hypnotized me that I was fluttering like a cock bird who was being slaughtered*" amply illustrates this fact. He was apparently aware of the deleterious as well as the restorative effect of music on himself, as well as on others. To thoroughly understand and appreciate this art, he studied vocal, instrumental (including percussion) music from maestros like Pyare Khan and Basat Khan. He learned the art of poetry from Qutub Ali Khan. With time, the king himself became an adept in *sitar* playing and *dhrupad.* He imbibed the finer nuances of *tabla* playing from Chote Khan, later named Anis-ud-Daula, who was assigned several administrative responsibilities later on in the Nawabi court.

Ghulam Raza, a recurrent personality in Wajid Ali's narrative, belonged to a family of musicians from Rampur. Before joining the Nawabi court at Lucknow, two sisters, Amman and Imaman had achieved fame in the households of the rich in Farrukhabad.

Awarded with the title, *Surur-e-Mehfil Waliyan*, their mother was named Majju and father was called Nathu. Their brothers were Ghulam Raza and Gehman, but addressed as Chacha Ghulam Nabi and Mamu Ghulam Haider. Ghulam Raza was an accomplished *sarangi* player and soon became a close confidante of the king. The family was given the job of training the *paris*, and the king himself would practice with the other students of Nathu Khan. But according to Wajid Ali, "he himself became such an adept that he left his teacher far behind." Ghulam Raza has been described as of short height with broad forehead and large eyes - respectful and carefree by nature. He also possessed tremendous physical strength. Ghulam Raza, Gehman Jaan, Chajju Khan and Sabit Ali would be present in the *Parikhana* for most of the day, and due to their presence, the festive atmosphere remained live. And in this way, the *paris* would also be trained and tutored. By Wajid Ali's own admission, he would himself be totally engrossed in acquiring musical skills all day long. Incidentally, the family were followers of the *Sunni* faith. However, Wajid Ali managed to convert Ghulam Raza to the *Shi'a* faith and honoured him with the title of Ghulam Ali Khan. Similarly Qutub Ali Khan was converted and honoured with the title of Ghulam Yadullah Khan and later, Qutub-ud-Daula Mufta-hul-Mulk. They were subsequently saddled with administrative posts, which was fodder to the British premise that "fiddlers and drummers" were ruling the roost in the court of Lucknow.

Did Wajid Ali actually believe that music was a potent force, which could be used to manipulate the thought processes of listeners in the audience? That vibrations generated from vocals and musical instruments could affect the cosmos and all within it, as a kind of supernatural phenomenon? As per his own admission, the king could make his audience "*cry as they laughed and laugh as they cried*." For him, music could be a sort of therapy for his own emotions as well as the emotions of others. As one pores through the pages of *Ishqnama*, it is evident that the prince / king loved to play games with his audience; sometimes he would perform from behind a curtain and enthral his audience. He would also disguise himself, and play incognito, all the while enjoying the dizzying effect that his music had on others.

Wajid Ali was never a conventional Islamic ruler. The Nawabi court at Lucknow had always been an unusual amalgam of religious syncretism and Lucknow's last king took this to another level of pantheism, unabashedly donning saffron and looking upon Lord Krishna as a role model. It is therefore no surprise that his *paris* spontaneously took upon the role of Lord Krishna's *gopis,* although most, if not all, were practicing Muslims, and quite orthodox, at that. As per established convention - as an offshoot of the Mughal court of Delhi, although an Islamic ruler could enjoy the pleasures of dance, music and poetry, it was taboo that he should personally engage in dance and music. It has never been established whether Wajid Ali himself danced as in a public performance. However, he was not above correcting the *paris* in person, if they made mistakes while performing. And this would require him to join the performers on-stage and demonstrate the correct steps and / or nuances of classical dance. With time, Wajid Ali became such an adept in the performing arts that he was no less than a maestro himself, an *ustad*, who had surpassed his teachers and instructors. His first book on musicology was *Saut-ul-Mubarak*, published in 1852 - 53 at Lucknow. It was written in *Farsi,* and drew upon the older texts, including one from the days of Asaf-ud-Daula, named *Usul al-Naghmat-e-Asafi*. The book was a detailed treatise on musicology, dealing particularly with the various nuances of *sur* (melody) as compared to *taal* (rhythm). It is said that there were seventeen hundred men possessing literary abilities and the same number of men of music, dance and drama in the court of the king (Ansari, 2014). Later, during his exile in Calcutta, he would produce music anthologies (in Urdu) titled *Najo, Dulhan, Bani* and *Chanchal Nāzanîn*. Another book, *Risala-e-Mausiqui* is attributed to the king, but it's existence as a separate piece of literature is unclear. Several classical ragas such as *Jogi, Juhi* and *Shah Pasand* have also been attributed to Wajid Ali. He was a prolific writer, which is evident from the fact that his book, *Bahar-e-Ulfat* had four thousand couplets and *Habat-e-Haidari* had three thousand couplets. He wrote *masnavis*, *ghazals, noha, salaam, qasida, qata, rubai* and *marsiya* with equal ease (Ansari, 2014). In his book *Bani*, Wajid Ali listed forty six books written by him, during his stay in *Metia Burz*. Of course, several were written after *Bani* also. *Annexure 1* has an indicative list of books written by Wajid Ali Shah during his lifetime. It has been purported that the ruler / ex-ruler never wrote by hand; he would recline on a couch and dictate to a transcriber. Apparently, he could dictate two different compositions simultaneously to two different transcribers. As expected, he was fluent in *Farsi*, Urdu and Hindustani, but not very proficient in Arabic. However, Khwaja Zain-ul-Abedin, who joined the ex-king's services in 1876 at *Metia Burz* reported that in old age, the king not only preferred to write on his own - he would also experiment with calligraphy and simple decorative motifs which he liked to draw on his manuscripts.

Wajid Ali Shah directed three *rahas* or "dance-dramas" during his rule that were based on his *masnavis*: *Darya-e-T'ashuq*, *Afsana-e-Ishq* and *Bahar-e-Ulfat*. There are no available scripts of the adaptations. The *masnawi Darya-e-T'ashuq* related the romance of the princess Ghazala and the son of the minister, Mehru. The staging of this story was witnessed by Wajid Ali Shah's paternal uncle Iqtidar-ud-Daula, who described the event in *Tarikh-e-Iqtidariya*:

"[This play] *was performed in 1267 Hijri (1850), after a preparation of one year. Somewhere someone presented the story of Ghazala Mahrukh, in service of the king. The king transformed it into verse and called it a masnavi. Spending several lakhs of rupees, he prepared a rahas out of it. The description of the first day of the jalsa is as follows: the preparations of the jalsa took place in the Farhat Manzil of Kaiserbagh and Wajid Ali Shah sent for all the princes. They all came into the Farhat Manzil and sat on chairs, and the king himself sat in front of everybody on a high chair... When the dance ended, an embroidered cushioned seat* *was brought out and put in place. One person, playing the king, came over and sat there. Then, all the women began to sing: "May the Life (*Light?*) of the World* (the king) *congratulate with the rahas"* ... *On the second day, in the same manner, Wajid Ali Shah came over and sat down, and all the princes sat on their respective chairs... that entire night was spent in the jalsa and in the early morning the rahas ended.. The drama had more than a hundred female performers with lavish costumes and a large numbers of musicians including sarangi players. The staging took place in several buildings: Farhat Manzil, Kaiser Manzil, Mashuq Manzil, amongst others in fourteen sessions over a month and ten days.*" All the specifics of this *rahas* were recorded with great detail by Wajid Ali Shah's uncle (Castro, 2016).

As described elsewhere, Wajid Ali's *Khas Mahal*, Alam Ara Begum was an accomplished poetess in her own right. Wajid Ali's *nom de plume* was *Akhtar* or *Akhtar Pia*, whereas the *begum* composed under the *takhallus* of *Alam.* Wajid Ali composed many forms of Hindustani classical music, including *dhrupad* and *khayal* but he was an authority on *thumris.* Ironically, it appears that *Khas Mahal* wrote more *thumris* than the king himself. Both were equally adept in composing *dhrupads* also. As with Wajid Ali, the queen was not averse to the use of Hindu motifs in her compositions. Her *dhrupad*s are unabashed invocations to Hindu deities. While Wajid Ali seemed fascinated with Lord Krishna, *Khas Mahal* tried to create a fusion between the Lord Rama at Ayodhya and the Nawabi court at Lucknow. She wrote primarily in Hindustani dialect and was also responsible for designing costumes for the *paris* in *Parikhana*. The royal couple's talent was not constrained during their exile at *Mẹtia Burz*, Calcutta and they continued with aplomb, despite the occasional strain in relationship between the two. But gradually, the effect of Bengali language and culture crept into their compositions.

Wajid Ali's interests also included the intricacies of dance forms, especially *kathak*. Sharar (Harcourt and Hussain, 1989) candidly stated that a Durga Prasad taught Wajid Ali how to dance. Earlier, *kathak* exponents of the oldest Rajasthani *gharana* had created the Lucknow *gharana* by integrating with classical dance forms of Awadh. One of the earliest exponents of the Lucknow *gharana* was Pandit Ishwari Prasad Mishra, whose grandson, Prakashji, had migrated to the court of Asaf-ud-Daula. Thakur Prasad, Durga Prasad and Maharaj Maanji were the sons of Prakashji.

However, Wajid Ali did not mention this in his own writings. In fact, he stated that he taught himself how to dance and soon became accomplished in it. But it is widely accepted that Wajid Ali Shah's blending of *kathak* with *thumri* was a significant development of the Lucknow *gharana,* wherein, the steps of *kathak* were accentuated with the lyrics of *thumri.* His contribution to this art form was the *rahas*, again based on the divine love (*Ras Leela*) between Krishna and Radha. He wrote *Radha Kanhaiya Ka Qissah* in 1843 in the Urdu language. In 1846, Wajid Ali staged a play based on the love story of Princess Ghazala, titled *Darya-e-Tashq*. In 1853, his *Afsana-e-Ishq* was produced. Subsequently, *Bahar-e-Ulfat* and several others followed. Several decades later, Wajid Ali produced thirty six *rahas* in his book, *Bani,* with exotic names such as *Mor Chhatri*, *Ghoongat*, *Salami*, *Chumak*, *Mor Pankhi* and *Mujra.* With time, the king slowly gravitated towards the role of director / producer of his musical soirees, from his early days of being the principal character / actor. The *Jalsakhana* of *Metia Burz*, Calcutta was a later *avatar* of Lucknow's now defunct *Parikhana,* with the same set of problems, and few more, e.g. financial constraints and the now aged king's increasingly querulous behaviour.

The reader might be inclined to wonder whether sex and eroticism were intimately related to music, dance and poetry in those times? Or were these merely different sides of the same coin, encompassing Lucknow's decadent Nawabi culture? In Lucknow's Nawabi court (before the 1856 annexation), these sides had become increasingly blurred and indistinct from each other. That the actions (and even appearance) of women (often low born) could elevate one to the dizzying heights of ecstasy, and then bring him down to despondency and depression, was aptly described by the ruler himself in *Ishqnama*. Most of the narrative concerned this aspect of the early life of Wajid Ali; if he was a musical and dance maestro, if he was an accomplished poet, then he was also a connoisseur of women. Wajid Ali was reported to have emphasised that, "*I have developed a certain amount of refinement in my nature, having breathed a thousand types of breaths in the company of Qutub Ali Khan* (his *sitar* tutor). *My heart would be remain morose without song and music, and I would not find a woman agreeable, if she was inconversant with these talents*." It is a moot point as to how women of various denominations, including professional courtesans, maid servants, dancers / singers, or *mut'ah* wives, could dominate the life of the king from his early childhood in Lucknow to his death at Calcutta at the age of sixty five years. *Ishqnama* has been described as Wajid Ali's "most explicit exposition on emotion and senses" (Davis, 2014). Written early in his lifetime, the narrative within was to serve as a cornerstone for expounding and elucidating the ruler's amorous adventures as well as his increasing skills and proficiency in the performing arts throughout his life. He had clearly stated in the narrative that, "*It may be emphasised here that this arrangement at Parikhana was not to encourage romance or lust; it was to promote and nurture musical training in those women who had the flair and talent for it.*" Wajid Ali had also written the following justification in the narrative titled *Jashn-e-Mahtabi*:

"*Kings have traditionally made full arrangements for the training of their female companions, resulting in the latter becoming highly trained in the arts and crafts. Notable among them have been Mohammad Shah (Rangila), King of Delhi, the Sultan of Bijapur, Adil Shah and other rulers, who trained beautiful and elegant women in music, raising their status as formal singers. Accordingly, this royal personage, following tradition, also arranged for the musical upbringing and schooling of several beautiful women, whose mere gestures could act like arrows, proving fatal for prospective lovers. The ribbons used to braid their hair resembled black serpents. Eyebrows were poisonous scorpions, ready to strike. Their singing was indeed divine. The soul would struggle to free itself from the body. On witnessing a dance performance, even a fire-worshipper would bow his head and prostate himself in reverence. The audience would be amazed on seeing the flashy and gorgeous dresses and beautiful ornaments. The planets would forget their orbits and plead to learn the nuances of dance of Indrasabha. Peacocks would be attendants. Just as day and night have a thousand nuances, these dancing girls too would exhibit novel dance forms, new musical compositions and contemporary styles, which gave succour to the soul. Arms would flutter like a fish out of water. Soon after I had given orders that their musical training should be completed in all respects, these paris attained such perfection and became such adepts, that one could consider them worthy of competing with maestros such as Tansen and Baiju*".

This reference to *Indrasabha*, the court of yet another God of the Hindu pantheon has been discussed later in this book. With his accession as king of Awadh, and the building of the *Kaiserbagh* palace complex, several musical dance dramas were staged, some lasting for more than a month, complete with ostentatious sets and dazzling costumes worn by the *paris*. Wajid Ali wrote unabashedly, "*The paris of my Parikhana had become so adept in their craft that the celestial nymphs from Lord Indra's court and famed fairies of the Caucasian mountains, would have faced a serious challenge. Each and every pari had the seductiveness to shatter the hearts of human spectators. And I could entirely perceive the proficiency therein. If I could free myself from one attractive seductress, I would get entangled in the mortal coils of another. Without them, even day-to-day activities would be colourless and devoid of pleasure.*" Thus, the king had managed to seamlessly create a magical and imaginary kingdom within his own real kingdom

Fig. 12: *Jogiya Mela*, with Wajid Ali Shah in the centre, *Ishqnama*.

(Llewellyn-Jones, 2014). The British, of course, were never invited to these gala events. An annual *Jogiya Mela*, where Wajid Ali dressed himself as a Hindi ascetic, clad in saffron robes, was held in the *Kaiserbagh* complex during 1853 - 1855, in the monsoon season. This *mela* (fair) was open to the public, with the attendees, perforce, being clad similarly. In fact, this practice seems to have stemmed from his birth and childhood, together with the prophecy of astrologers, described earlier. Strangely the full colour painted illustration (Fig. 12) of the *Jogiya Mela* as depicted in the *Ishqnama* shows the king (in the centre) clad in green-blue and other participants clad in various shades of pink, red, saffron and green.

Abdul Halim "Sharar" (1989), known as the "cultural biographer of Lucknow" was born at Lucknow in 1860. By then, Nawabi rule followed by the events of 1857 were already over, and the people of Lucknow were trying to adjust to a new normal, under British masters and *ta'aluqdars* (landed barons) from the hinterlands of Awadh. In this depressing scenario, Abdul Halim lived out the first nine years of his life in Lucknow, before moving to Calcutta to join his father, who had earlier accompanied Wajid Ali Shah to *Metia Burz* in 1856. Sharar returned to Lucknow in 1879. An unabashed admirer of Lucknow with personal experience of life in the court of the exiled king, he poured out his feelings in a series of articles which appeared in *Dil Gudaz*, titled *Hindustan Mein Mashriqi Tamaddun Ka Akhri Namuna* or *Guzasta Lakhnau*. Surprisingly, he wrote deprecatingly about Wajid Ali:

"*Wajid Ali Shah could not outdo Navab Mirza* (Nawab Mirza Shauq, a contemporary poet, whose romantic poems describing beautiful veiled women, had become a cause célèbre in erotic literature) *in the realm of poetry, so he decided to surpass him by proclaiming to the world his unchaste predilections, thoughts and deeds. He even had no hesitation in showing shamefully low taste and in using obscene language. He would fall in love with female palanquin bearers, courtesans, domestic servants and women who came in and out of the palace; in short with hundreds of women, and because he was heir to the throne, he had great success with his love affairs. The shameful accounts of which can be read in his poems, writings and books. His character, therefore, appears to be one of the most dubious in all the records of history.*"

3

Tawa'if and *Mut'ah*: A Study in Contrasts

"Umrao Jaan" remains the most famous courtesan of Lucknow in public memory, but ironically, she was but a fictional character from the pen of Mirza Mohammad Hadi "Ruswa." Ruswa was born in Lucknow in 1857, and like Sharar, had missed out the personal experience of the city's Nawabi culture. Nevertheless, his first fictional Urdu novel, *Umrao Jaan Ada*, published in 1905, became a landmark in describing the life of a Lucknow courtesan during Nawabi rule. Unlike Prem Chand's *Shatranj Ke Khilari* filmed under the same name (Satyajit Ray, 1977) and Ruskin Bond's *A Flight of Pigeons* (produced as the film *Junoon* by Shyam Benegal, 1978), the Bollywood films on *Umrao Jaan* (Muzaffar Ali, 1981 and JP Dutta, 2006), although depicting the Nawabi period of Lucknow, made no political statements. And yet, together with the earlier film, *Pakeezah* (Kamal Amrohi, 1972), a certain visual imagery, through music, drama and glamour, was created for the public eye, regarding the courtesan culture of Lucknow of yore. Recently, Khatun (2020) has argued that these created an imaginary notion of Muslim women, who were represented to be well versed in the art of seduction, and yet subservient, by ignoring the liberated identity of *tawa'ifs*. In short, creating public awareness about the *tawa'if* through audio-visual medium was OK but creating a somewhat misleading, imaginary notion through normative majoritarian gender discourse was not OK.

So has the Lucknow *tawa'if* come a long way since the days of Wajid Ali Shah? According to popular sentiment, the king had left a lasting contribution on the courtesan culture or *tawa'if bazi*, but this premise appears to be patently erroneous.

Courtesan culture in Lucknow seems to have been a gradual social phenomenon, due to several factors. Itinerant entertainers (*mirasi*), composed of musicians and dancers who were traditionally community-based, existed during Mughal times, often employed professionally by the Mughal court or even army. Communities of these entertainers resided in *mohallas* (settlements) across Rohilkhand, around the towns of Shahjahanpur, Rampur, Bulandshahr, Najibabad and Muzaffarnagar and would periodically or permanently visit Lucknow for work. This ethnically and artistically diverse group of musicians who sang, played instruments such as *sarangi*, *sarod* and *tabla*, were socially and culturally bunched together in Lucknow, mostly under the single category *dhari*, the same occupational label previously used to categorise military musicians in the Mughal administration (McNeil, 2009). Danish Iqbal, a historian and academic, explained that the word *tawa'if* was the derivative of the Urdu word *taifi*, meaning "a travelling troupe." Some etymologists believe that *tawa'if* comes from the Arabic word *tauf* or *tawaf*, which means circling around, roaming or circumambulation. The number of women in the *tawa'if* community for the districts of North-West Provinces and Awadh was estimated at 473 in 1881 and at 1,4575 in 1891 (Chanda *et al*, 2021). As the Mughal court weakened, the migration towards Lucknow became markedly significant. Also, in those days, entertainment (both public and private) and not prostitution was the main focus. Awadh's *Shi'a* court was distinctly more permissive and indulgent, including matters of religion. *Tawa'ifs* not only participated actively in reciting *marsiyas* (reading of elegies related to Muharram) and participating in *soz-khwani* (recitation of dirges related to Muharram), many financially sound *tawa'ifs* also built *Imambaras*, where *majlis* (religious congregations) could be held. All this could not have been possible, without the active patronage and encouragement, which the *tawa'ifs* received from Awadh nobility.

In addition to its liberal rulers, Awadh also had its fair share of *begums*, who wielded considerable administrative and financial authority in their own right (Santha, 1980; Sarkar, 2015). Notable ones among these were Nawab Begum (wife of Safdarjang), Bahu Begum (wife of Shuja-ud-Daula), Badshah Begum (wife of Ghazi-ud-Din Haider) and Mallika Kishwar (wife of Amjad Ali Shah). A cloistered life in the *zenana*, did not deter them from deciding and implementing social and religious codes; Badshah Begum was particularly known for inventing rigorous religious practices and forcefully implementing them. *Khas Mahals* often had extensive *jagirs* which they administered through trusted *khwajasara*s (transgenders) and collected substantial revenue. They founded localities and markets, planted gardens, built mosques and *Imambaras*, patronised authors, artisans and engaged in playing games like *chaupar* (Qureshi, 2003). Indeed, during Nawabi rule, Awadh did not lack in female emancipation, from the ruling elites in their palaces to the *tawa'ifs* in their *kothas*.

Apart from religious and cultural contribution (in terms of song and dance), the *tawa'ifs* led a dissolute life, described in detail by Mahmud Aslam (2017). Young girls would join the profession, either on a hereditary or community basis, or simply due to financial constraints. They would be given a new name, and trained by the seniors in dance, music, social etiquette, art of seduction and giving sexual pleasure. Males from various social strata, from nobility to working classes frequented the brothels, and were received and entertained as per their financial status. Marriages between the client and *tawa'if* were rare but not unheard of. It must be emphasised here that all such liaisons between client and *tawa'if* did not necessarily conclude with sex. Other than the religious implications described above, the social interaction between the client and the *tawa'if* could have a purely cultural motive also. With time, as more and more *tawa'ifs* became exponents of song, dance and poetry, artistic entertainment became the norm, rather than providing sexual services. The *tawa'ifs* enjoyed the social position of an elite performing community throughout the 1800s (Oldenburg, 1990) and were engaged in several types of performance arenas: in court assemblies organised by nobility, in private gatherings arranged by elite members of the public, and of course, in their own *kothas* (Walker, 2010; Chanda, 2021).

Coming back to the Nawabi court, we see that the concept of the harem for the rulers became entrenched from Shuja-ud-Daula's reign onwards (Qureshi, 1982). Shuja's special inclination towards women led to a large scale exodus of prostitutes and dancing girls from Delhi to Faizabad and there were hardly any corner or street, where they did not reside. Some such women also came from Bihar. None knew when the fit of sensuousness would engulf the Nawab, and hence the tents of the pretty women, duly guarded by soldiers, always accompanied him, wherever he went. It was also reported that he had opened a market at Faizabad, which was exclusively run by pretty women. This set a very bad precedent for Awadh (Srivastava, 1961; Qureshi, 2003). Asaf-ud-Daula had a substantial harem; he was a great lover of dancing girls and prostitutes. Even the dancing girls Bhagya and Salaru were his great favourites (Qureshi, 2003) and he did not hesitate to travel with his women folk (and animals) while going for war. A hilarious account given by Thomas Twining, a civil servant of the EIC was as follows: "*The Nabob himself was still absent from Lucnow*(sic)*, having with him more than a hundred of the many hundred ladies of his seraglio, and many thousand pigeons, a fact which left no surprise that his Highness should have been so far in the rear, when the army of Sir Robert Abercromby fought the Rohillahs...*" Wazir Ali too was not above indulging in sexual orgies during his brief tenure as a Nawab, and later life at Benaras (Qureshi, 2003).

So did the women of "the profession" enter the harems of the rulers of Awadh as wives? It appears that women of lowly backgrounds did (e.g., Nasir-ud-Din Haider and Amjad Ali Shah), but not from the courtesan community, till the ascension of

Wajid Ali Shah. In *Ishqnama,* Wajid Ali mentioned a number of courtesans who successfully entered his establishment, some even acquiring the title of *mahal*, i.e. having given birth to a son. These included Waziran, Haidri (Sultan Pari), Yasmin Pari, Izzat Pari, Hur Pari, Mehboob (Mahrukh Pari), Munna (Imtiaz Pari), Chunni (Dilruba Pari), Ganna (Sarfaraz Pari), Sardar Pari, Mashuq Pari, Hazrat Mahal (Mehak Pari), Jaan Ilahi (Dildar Pari), Karambaksh Wali (Amir Pari), Sukhbadan Wali (Wazir Pari), Umrao Khanum (Sikander Begum), Bakshi, Ali Jaan, Amir Baksh, Bandi Umda Wali and Umrao Begum. Of course, this list spanned only the youth of Wajid Ali, as described in the *Ishqnama*. He would continue to acquire *mut'ah* wives all through his life, even when he was an exiled king at Calcutta.

Mut'ah denotes a private and verbal temporary marriage contract that is practiced in *Shi'a* Islam, in which the duration of the marriage and the *mehar* are specified and agreed upon in advance. It is a private contract made in a verbal or written format. A declaration of the intent to marry and an acceptance of the terms are required as in other forms of marriage in Islam. Partners who engage in *mut'ah* must do so freely, without any form of duress. The woman, therefore, has no claim for maintenance, and the two do not inherit from one another unless there is a previous agreement on these matters. Any children from a *mut'ah* union go with the father. No extension of the *mut'ah* is permitted, but cohabitation may be resumed if a new agreement is reached with new compensation for the woman. The marriage automatically dissolves at the end of the stated period. Thereafter, regardless of how short the marriage was, the woman has to observe sexual abstinence for the length of two menstruation cycles. This is to identify a child's legitimate father, in case she is pregnant. Unfortunately, men and women are not par in a *mut'ah* union. A man can simultaneously enter into multiple *mut'ah* marriages, but a woman can have only one temporary husband at a time. A married man can have a *mut'ah* marriage, but not a married woman. The rule of sexual abstinence, after a *mut'ah* marriage is over, does not apply to men.

Western scholars have often stated that while *nikah* marriage is for procreation, *mut'ah* marriages are for sexual gratification, or simply to legalise prostitution. While it is beyond the scope of this book to analyse Islamic jurisprudence, there is no doubt that Wajid Ali scrupulously adhered to the tenets of *mut'ah* marriages all through his lifetime, inasmuch as his contact with the female sex was concerned. His *mut'ah* wives could be grouped into three categories: the *mahals*, who had given birth to a son, the *begums*, who had not produced any offspring and the *khilawati,* who were actually domestic help, but married to the king. The *begums* were maximum in number; Wajid Ali's religious principles prohibited him from interacting with any woman, unless she was married to him. Hence his maids too were married to him in *mut'ah* wedlock, although it did not give them any special privileges as such. As discussed elsewhere, the ex-king could dispose off his *mut'ah* wives quite abruptly and ruthlessly, leading to conflicts with British officials, who were unable to understand or appreciate the religious principles involved in such bizarre actions of the ex-king. Wajid Ali felt fully justified with his approach towards his *mut'ah* partners, and felt that the British were encroaching upon his rights and privileges, due to him as an Islamic (ex) ruler. However, it must be admitted that by giving *mut'ah* status to even *tawa'ifs,* he had introduced a new dimension to the respectability of courtesans becoming wives (albeit temporary), and enhancing their social status a few niches higher. But the bubble was about to burst.

Post 1857, the British actively discouraged the *tawa'ifs* from practicing their professions in Lucknow and elsewhere. There was a sneaky belief that *tawa'ifs* had played a key role in the 1857 resistance movement by Indian freedom fighters. In any case, the Nawabi court and the affluent gentry had been decimated. With the Cantonment Act of 1864, the British sought to regulate sexual services being provided to British soldiers, through segregations, registrations and health checks. Many *tawa'ifs* did turn to prostitution, few became concubines of the rich. Others honed their musical and dancing talents and managed to eke out a living in the changed circumstances. As discussed in Chapter I, photography had become popular from the late 1850s onwards. Other than Abbas Ali, Chote Mian (the architect of *Hussainabad* and *Kaiserbagh*) and Mushkoor-ud-Daula were active during the period, possibly having access to the royal *zenana* also. Like Abbas Ali, Mushkoor-ud-Daula too photographed *tawa'ifs,* possibly from 1865 onwards. Another photographer, whose mention crops up is Musaddi Lal. These later photographic collections listed Lucknow courtesans like Miss Biggan, Miss Mulka Jan, Miss Mahemuneer, Miss Mooshtari Jan, Miss Noor Jahan and others. In a changing society with a mixed morality, where most of the Indian social reformers had received an English education, the courtesans became a symbol of decadence. They were portrayed as the sinful practitioners of the *ars amandi*, even though many of them were solely dedicated to the performing arts and recognized as top *khayal*, *thumri*, *tappa* and *ghazal* singers as well as *kathak* dancers. It is hardly surprising that they were the first artists to be recorded by the Chief Recorder of the Gramophone Company, Fred W. Gaisberg, who reached Calcutta in 1902 (Bautze, 2009).

In the ex-king's court at Calcutta, the situation became even more critical, due to lack of finances and the king's bludgeoning family liabilities. After his death in September 1887, the late king was survived by two *nikah* and two hundred and fifty *mut'ah* wives, together with their offspring and dependents. The task of providing for all these dependents in a fair manner, and simultaneous disposal of the ex-king's estate was no easy task. Nevertheless, it was done, although controversy and conflict continued to beleaguer the inheritance for a very long time.

Abode of Fairies

Badshah Wajid Ali Shah, Unidentified Artist

4

The *Parikhana*

*B*e it known to all that the Lord of the World has granted to every man, the boon of love and the right to bloom in this garden of eternal spring. My sorrow has also emerged from this rose water, a dirge arising and becoming an agonizing part of my fate. Accordingly, I am narrating the story of my of love and passion, which I have endured from boyhood till present. At present, I am entering the twenty-sixth year of my life, having experienced a surfeit of betrayal in my lifetime.

Rahiman

When I was eight years old, a woman named Rahiman was appointed as my maid. She was around forty five years of age. She would be available at my service all the time. One day while I was sleeping, she started teasing and molesting me. Because I was a child, I tried to run off in fear. But she stopped me, by threatening that she would get me punished by the *maulvi*[1], who was my teacher. I was worried about my predicament, and from that day onwards, she would regularly violate me. This continued till I was ten years old. After that, God knows where she went, I don't remember anything.

Since I was interested in the pleasures of love from an early age, I often lamented at the plight of true lovers, and berate insensitive paramours.

Amiran

In those days, a woman named Amiran was maid-in-waiting to my esteemed mother. She was around thirty four years old, having a wheatish complexion and a voluptuous body. Her left eye had a white mark. She would always be garishly dressed, but in an attractive manner. Being of loose morals, she knew how to act seductively, thereby enticing males with ease. Although she worked on a monthly salary of four rupees, she lived a life of luxury. In fact, it was obvious that she could manage her lifestyle through illicit means.

Once, all my relatives had gone to the palace of King Nasir-ud-Din Haider[2] on the occasion of the circumcision ceremony of Munna Jaan[3]. Seeing the entire household empty, that woman came to my bed where I was sleeping and touched me intimately. In fact, I had some weakness for her also. Because of this, I was not perturbed at her advances, and pretended to be asleep, so as not to disturb her. In this way, I passively enjoyed her ministrations and intoxicating touch. She remained in my memories as an erotic dream, till I was eleven years old.

Banno Saheb

When I attained the age of eleven years, I would cast loving looks at every beautiful woman I saw, and would try to draw their attention towards me. I would be enamoured by their coyness and would enjoy their pleasing coquetry. In those days, there was a black woman by the name of Musammi Banno Saheb, whose father, a negro, was named Ghaliban Shaidi Sultan, but whose mother was an Indian. This woman was in the service of my mother, as a maid. She was married to a man named Mirza Jaan. For quite some time, I was entranced by her and she would always be in my heart and mind. But it was a difficult task, as she was an intelligent woman, who was proud of her womanhood. Because of this, she would tactfully avoid my advances.

Eventually, I gave her the nick-name *Dogana*[4] and would sit near her and talk to her, simply to assuage my feelings towards her. The motive behind this intimacy and attachment was nothing but to have a love affair with her.

Banno Saheb was around twenty three years old. She was dark skinned, with a well-proportioned body, short height, beautiful teeth and lips, thin eyebrows, mischievous eyes, sharp nose, wavy hair, and soft fingers. She was barely literate, but could read the *Koran* and Urdu, fluently. She was an expert seamstress and could play *Ganjfa.*[5] She was also virtuous and an excellent companion to my most esteemed mother. Banno had one brother and four sisters in her family. The brother was named Shaidi Ahmed Khan, who had a concubine called Waziran. Waziran had served in the court of Nasir-ud-Din Haider and also knew me, but she was staying in the home of Shaidi. Apparently, they did not share a cordial relationship with each other.

Banno had four sisters, one of whom was called Haji Khanum, who was younger to Banno and also married. One day, Haji was on a visit to her elder sister, in the house of my esteemed mother.

Haji Khanum

I was sitting with my grandmother, Mariam Makani, during the rainy season, in the month of *Saawan*. I saw a woman who was around twenty two years of age; attractive and lively. Tall bearing, stately figure, bright eyes, framed with light eyebrows and a narrow waist. Eyes tinged with green and black pupils. Lips and teeth to die for; perfectly proportioned hands and feet; wavy hair and lips layered with sweet *missi* (dentifrice), hennaed hands, ears adorned with shiny stone tops, which cast a brightness on her cheeks; she was bathed in *itr* (perfume / essence), which assailed the senses. Carrying a five year old child, she gracefully came and paid obeisance to my grandmother. It was love at first sight for me. My feelings for her were on fire, just like a *hammam*[6] boils with the fire of wood. I lost my patience and self-control. The memories of Banno Saheb also fled from my heart. To be honest, I became her ardent admirer, and would silently beseech, "Ya Allah, if only I had been a bird, singing thousands songs in praise of this youthful beauty, having the appearance of angels and beauty of fairies." Because she had come recently, my relatives kept a strict watch over her. I could not achieve anything, other than admiring her beauty from a distance. In this manner, the days and nights passed and I remained forlorn. Since I was not familiar with the nuances of love, I remained in this state of internal turmoil. But I did not confide with anyone as regards my painful state of affairs. Eventually, Haji Khanum came to know of my infatuation, and she finally relented to my unrequited love for her.

Haji Khanum had a tutor called Imami Khanum, who was an exceedingly ugly woman. She was around forty years of age and she had also taught my sister. I used her for conveying messages to Haji Khanum, as a result of which, I came to know about the latter in detail. But Imami carried a wrong impression of herself. Despite being physically unattractive, she considered herself to be an unparalleled beauty. Also, she did not pay heed to the fact that she was a tutor of Haji Khanum, and being my confidant, she tried to ensnare me with her charms. Although I did not pay heed to her wiles - for the sake of Haji Khanum, I gave her my regards and paid due attention to her. My actions made her think mistakenly that I had yielded to her coquettishness, and that I was in the throes of her love, just as a fish dies out of water.

I was always very respectful towards my elders, and in such matters, I would take special precautions. Imami proved to be appropriate for the task at hand. Consequently, myself and Haji Khanum accepted Imami as part of our lifestyle, despite the latter's ugly countenance and undesirable activities. Both of us would not have achieved our objective of illicit love, without Imami's help. Honestly speaking, not a moment would pass, in which I would not suffer from the fiery throes of passion for Haji. She was also equally enamoured by me. Many a time, because of her distance from me - night and day, she would weep in her home. However, I would not have to suffer this parting for long, as on some pretext or the other, she would leave her home and return.

Like Laila Majnu[7], whenever we two sat together, we would pass the time in delightful conversation. With talks of love and passion, we would try to assuage our feelings. Sometimes Haji Khanum would talk bitterly, which would cause me anguish. Sometimes, she would also mention her husband, which hurt me. But the moment she realised my predicament, she would change the topic and talk of love and passion once more, which would clear the gloominess in my heart.

A maid named Ilahi Khanum, who was actually the sister-in-law of Haji Khanum, served under Banno Saheb. Call it a coincidence, but in those days, she was also infatuated with me. In brief, my passion for Haji Khanum lasted till I was about thirteen to fourteen years of age. Because she was married and her home was in Faizabad, she could not stay with us for long. When we finally parted, she gifted me a ring and a few pieces of ivory jewellery, which, although unwilling, I accepted as divine gifts, and bade her farewell.

Marriage

My parents started contemplating about my marriage, when I reached the age of fifteen years. After considerable thought, it was decided that I would marry Munir-ud-Daula's daughter (who now holds the title of Tajdar Bahu, as wife of my brother, Mirza Sikandar Hashmat Bahadur). But due to some reason, I did not accept this marriage proposal. After this, the daughter of Saif-ud-Daula Bahadur (who was *chakladar*[8] in Gonda-Bahraich) was found to be suitable for me. Negotiations were on, but some issues arose as a result of which, the wedding got delayed interminably and ultimately could not materialise. After this, marriage negotiations started with Wazir (who was actually my aunt) for her daughter's hand. Wazir whole-heartedly accepted the proposal, but her daughter suffered from leprosy – a fact which she had chosen to hide from us. So, naturally the marriage could not take place. Eventually, due to the efforts and goodwill of Jani Khanum (who was the *muh boli*[9] daughter of my grandmother, Anjum-Nisa Begum), the marriage proposal for daughter of late Ali Khan Bahadur[10] was conveyed to us. Since her's was a highly reputed family, I gave my consent for the same, and my parents were also overjoyed with the proposal. Accordingly, the *manje ki rasm*[11] was held on 15 *Shaban*, 1253 *Hijr* (Islamic calendar)[12].

However, it was God's will that the paternal aunt of my bride-to-be expired during that period. My uncle Nasir-ud-Daula Nawab Mirza Asghar[13] Ali's elder son, Mumtaz-ud-Daula, also died during the same period.

As a result of all this, my wedding ceremony could not take place on the designated date, and I was forced to be garbed in the clothes of the *manje* (yellow coloured, see above) ceremony for a full two months, as a result of which, they had become soiled and dirty. Chanting the name of Allah, the formalities were ultimately completed, and my wedding took place, accompanied by unusually lavish festivities.

My marital relations remained convivial during the first five months of our marriage.

Takht Nashini[14] of Hazrat Firdaus Manzil

Barely five months had passed after my marriage when Nasir-ud-Din Haider left for his heavenly abode. After this, my (late) grandfather, Nasir-ud-Daula Bahadur Firdaus Manzil[15] was crowned and he took over the reigns of the kingdom. Accordingly, all persons were honoured as per their rank and status. My father[15] was given the title of *Wali Ahad*[16]. The monthly allowances of members of the family were suitably enhanced, but he deprived me and my wife of his generosity. Maybe he thought that I would ultimately succeed my father, and rule over the kingdom in due course of time, and that is why he chose not to be generous with me. I can only theorise about this.

Seeing the situation, and in a bid to assuage my hurt feelings, my father, Amjad Ali Shah, granted me an allowance of rupees five hundred a month, and rupees four hundred a month to my wife.

During this time, I would surreptitiously flirt with the maidservants in my household. My wife started resenting these activities of mine. Consequently, she dismissed some of the maidservants, and made elaborate arrangements for keeping an eye on me. But I was helpless against my amorous nature, and would pass days and nights, lost in erotic dreams.

Birth of Mirza Nausherwan Qadr Bahadur

Barely a year had passed with my father as *Wali Ahad* when we were blessed with a royal son, whom we named as Mirza Nausherwan Qadr Bahadur. My grandfather, Hazrat Firdaus Manzil (reigning king, Mohammad Ali Shah) was overjoyed at this news and bestowed upon me several honorific titles *viz*. Nazim-ud-Daula Fakhrul Mulk Mohammad Wajid Ali Khan Bahadur Sailaté Jung. My son was named as Nausherwan Qadr Bahadur. After two or three months, my title was changed to Mirza Khurshid Mohammad Wajid Ali Shah.

Birth of Mirza Falakh Bahadur

In *1255 Hijr*, my second son was born, who was named as Mirza Falakh Qadr Bahadur[17], by my father, Amjad Ali. At the time of his birth, I was seventeen years of age.

Because I was in the peak of youth during this period, I felt that I should be spending the spring-time of my life in the company of beautiful women, pleasing to the senses. But due to obvious restrictions, I could not fulfil my pursuits freely. Finally, I decided on a ploy of appointing beautiful women as maidservants, and secretly engage in amorous activities with them. With this thought in mind, my restlessness was somewhat reduced. Consequently, as a step in this direction, I appointed a woman named Moti Khanum as a maid, who was doe-eyed, with a curvaceous body and wheatish complexion. She was playful, yet cunning. Her eyes were a bit disfigured due to small-pox. She had earlier entertained in the court of the late Nasir-ud-din Haider. It was no secret that the sole purpose of her appointment was to comfort me and to help me in fulfilling my secret desires.

But this action of mine was not appreciated by my *begum*, and she raised a hue and cry over it, as a result of which, Moti Khanum was dismissed, and I had to face the wrath of my esteemed father, who had me put under house arrest for some time.

Love for Moti Khanum

After this episode, I became a recluse and turned to poetry to assuage my feelings. However, I got no release from my pent-up emotions. Due to my father's anger against me, I became listless and apathetic. When he ultimately came to know about my condition, he ordered that the woman be brought back and handed over to me, with the condition that she would not stay in the same household, but live elsewhere. In fact, I had threatened to desist from partaking in food and water. I believe that the royal decree was a result of my protest. Immediately after this, Moti Khanum was brought in my presence.

Because obedience to parents' wishes is the prime duty for any offspring, I removed that woman from my presence and respectfully informed my father that my actions could not be against his wishes. After all this, I bid farewell to Moti Khanum. Now that my esteemed father has ascended to the heavens and I became king of Awadh, I could do whatever I wanted, yet I have most respectfully kept my promise made to my (late) father. I was merely eighteen years old when all this happened in my life. I developed a taste for *shayari* and wrote two compilations of *ghazals* and three *masnavis* as a token of my love for Moti Khanum. But I did not share the turmoil in my heart with anyone. To be honest, I was so consumed in the agony of my unrequited love that I was alive for namesake only.

After this incident, I never looked at my wife with love, which deeply pained her. Many a time, she tried to enquire about my welfare and know the cause of my aloofness. But I remained silent, and did not reply to any of her queries. Because she was a very intelligent woman, eventually she understood that she herself was responsible for all this. She also realised that she should keep me content, and by going against my wishes, it was not possible to lead a happy life. Eventually, she started telling me that she regretted her actions, if I was hurt in any manner and in future, I was free to love any woman whom I pleased. Because this was the crux of the problem, I replied that if she felt that way, it was alright with me[18].

Mirza Kaiwan Qadr Bahadur

My wife was blessed with a third child, who at this time, is the *Wali Ahad* of the kingdom[19]. My father, Amjad Hazrat Firdaus Manzil was much pleased at this and granted the title of Mirza Kaiwan Qadr Bahadur to the child.

A Love Affair with Saheb Khanum

In those days, my eyes fell on Musammi Saheb Khanum, a married woman and singer, who was employed in the household of Janab Qibla Walid Majid Hazrat Suraiya Jah. She was around thirty two years of age, having fair, reddish complexion, short height, broad face, shining eyes, a playful demeanour and undone hair, resting coquettishly on her shoulders. She was an adept in singing, playing music and also card games. She was a mother of two or three daughters. We both fell in love with each other. It came to pass that she could not sleep at nights, without first seeing my face. All the time, she would sit near me and either play cards, or engage in song and music. She would admirably sing the latest ghazals composed by me. Out of those ghazals, the first verse was as follows:

The progression of love has now stepped in
I was harmed, but let love flourish

I would give her few rupees daily, which she would accept whole-heartedly, and bring wrapped *paan*[20] for me, made by herself. If, by chance, she did not see me for sometime, she would run around, searching for me impatiently. If I was outdoors, she would watch me for hours through the trellis[21] of the door. Or climb on the terrace and exchange looks with me. In short, she could not spend a moment without seeing me.

Although my wife was aware of my romance with Saheb Khanum, she was like, "a burnt child dreads the fire." Accepting it as God's will, she chose to remain quiet. Saheb Khanum got so carried away in her love for me that once she took a metal part of my *sitar*[22] and heated it till it became glowing red. She then burned her left thigh with it. After being treated and bandaged, she limped to me, which made me ask the reason from her. To this, she replied, "Unfortunately you did not apply salve on me." I enquired, "But why would you require salve on yourself?" She replied, "I want salve to be applied on my thigh. If you don't consider it below your dignity, please do apply some on me, so my wound can heal." I then observed curiously that her left thigh was indeed inflamed. After this episode, our relations became like *Laila Majnu.* This continued for a year.

Birth and Death of Murtaza Begum

I was blessed with a daughter when I was just nineteen years of age. She was named Murtaza Begum Tazviz. But it was God's will that she died within forty days of her birth. It was during that period that my esteemed father, Amjad Ali Shah became king of the kingdom. Saheb Khanum's love also peaked during this period.

When my *begum* came to know about my affair with Saheb Khanum, she asked me one day, if my present love affair had my consent. I replied, "Why do you concern yourself with the affairs of others? What is written in my fate will happen. Albeit, I would have been grateful to you if you had selected a woman for me."

My *begum* was an extremely intelligent woman, well aware of the prevailing situation. Thus, without wasting any time, she started inviting other women to work as maids.

A Love Affair With Umda Begum

A woman named Umda Begum joined as a maid in my *begum's* household. She was a fine woman, around twenty seven years old; fair complexioned, proportioned figure, an expert in playing card games. She had been previously in the service of Nasir-ud-Din Haider, after whose demise, she was forced to seek employment elsewhere. I liked Umda Begum from the moment I first saw her. Gradually, a passion for her filled my heart. She also responded whole-heartedly to my ardour. In fact, her love for me surpassed my love for her. When Saheb Khanum and Umda Begum became acquainted with each other, a feeling of anger and jealousy started developing between them. Their mutual hatred for each other reached such heights that I had to sever relations with Saheb Khanum. Another reason why my relations with Saheb Khanum were not advisable was that she had been a maid of my esteemed father. Moreover, she was a married woman, whose husband was still around.

Nanhi Begum

During that time, three sisters were working in the household of my father. The eldest was named Haidri Begum, the middle was Muhammadi Begum and the youngest was Nanhi Begum. These three sisters were the maternal grand daughters of Mir Insha Khan, who were *zakiras*, reciting during *majlis*[23]. Nanhi Begum closely resembled a woman, known as Sarfaraz, who was actually a brothel keeper, whom I had seen during the marriage festivities of the (late) Mohammad Ali Shah's younger brother. At that time, she would have been seventeen – eighteen years old, and I was also of similar age. Since she was immersed in music, and I had also developed an interest in music and dance from a young age,

I fell in love with her charms. But she did not reciprocate, and neither did I send her any message of love, out of fear of my elders.

In short, when I saw Nanhi Begum so closely resembling Sarfaraz, I was attracted to her immensely. But she did not respond to my overtures. She regarded my love as a teenage infatuation. If I did come across her in solitude, and would try to express my feelings, she would tease me by saying, "I had been waiting for you for so long. Where were you at that time?" and would run off.

When Saheb Khanum was removed due to Umda Begum, the former regretted her disobedience. In fact, she had indulged in certain activities which were wholly objectionable to me. Moreover, I had offered to accommodate her and her two daughters in my household, provided she divorced her husband. But she paid no heed, as a result of which, I removed her from the scene. I could not think of any alternative. Other reasons were also there for her removal. She is still alive and is a maidservant to one of my wives.

After my break-up with Saheb Khanum, my love affair with Umda Begum touched dizzying heights. But secretly, I was smitten with Nanhi Begum also. I tried my level best to prevent Nanhi Begum from knowing about my relations with Umda Begum, and also keep Umda Begum unaware of the fact that I was head-over-heels in love with Nanhi Begum. But, secretly, both were well aware of each other. And the same situation arose, which had come to pass between Moti Khanum and Umda Begum. But due to her extreme attachment with me, Umda Begum did not create a similar chaotic situation. Although due to mutual ill-feeling, both had expressed their wish to leave my services and work elsewhere. But my *mahal*[24] neither let them quit, nor did she allow them to go back to their respective homes.

Takht Nashini[14] of Hazrat Jannat Makan

My esteemed father, Amjad Ali Shah occupied the throne (of his forefathers) of Awadh as *Badshah* (King). Through God's grace,

I was declared as *Wali Ahad* (heir apparent) of the kingdom. After this, I gave thought to the idea that I could marry Umda Begum and make her my queen. Her extreme devotion and her services for me had created a place in my heart for her. I loved her so intensely that barring my sleeping hours, and the time spent in my father's presence, the rest of each day was spent with her. Our love affair was like Laila Majnu and Shirin Farhad[25]. Although Nanhi Begum was aware of my condition, she desired that I should marry her too, and make her my *mahal*. This indicates that she was greedy, and perhaps felt that she should not miss a golden opportunity (of marrying into royalty).

Nanhi Begum was a dignified, pious woman, adept in reciting *marsiya*[26]. She was fair complexioned, of average height, having fine eyebrows, and small eyes… she was a widow, with a three year old daughter, named Ahmadi. After the death of her husband, she had been employed by my mother for reciting *marsiya*. Finally, with time, she admitted her passion for me but the glory and fortunes of Umda Begum was at its peak then. Consequently, the magic of Nanhi Begum did not work.

As a result of my affair with Umda Begum, the fire of jealousy and enmity was stoked in the heart of my *begum*, *Khas Mahal*. Her world was full of darkness, but as per a Hindustani proverb, *dariya mein rehkar magarmach se bair*[27], she kept quiet and remained helpless.

Preparations for my marriage with Umda Begum were in full swing, with all the accompanying accoutrements, *viz*. silver vessels and plates bearing costly clothes, gold ornaments and jewellery. After our marriage, she was given the title of Nawab Khurd Mahal. Her fortunes were on a high, like a star illuminating the whole world. However, after all this, the old adage, *char din ki chandni, fir andheri raat*[28] came true. Nanhi Begum remained covetous of Umda Begum, and hoped that I should free myself from the latter's charms, and marry her. In the end, I could not remain oblivious of her charms, because she tried various means to attract my attention towards her. Once she climbed on the bridge of the *Chattar Manzil* palace, which faced the Gomti river, and announced her desire to commit suicide. I leapt forward and holding her hand, told her that such actions were wholly unbecoming and undesirable on her part. That she would achieve nothing except disappointment and notoriety for her actions. In this way, I prevented her from taking an extreme step. During this time, her daughter had also died. Eventually, just after one-and-half months of my marriage with Umda Begum, I married Nanhi Begum also, who was given the title Nishat Mahal Nanhi Begum. She was given jewellery and costly dresses as per her new status. Unfortunately her good fortune lasted for fifteen days[29] only.

Nighar Mahal

It was the monsoon season. One day, the sky was overcast with dark clouds and it was drizzling slightly. The cool breeze blowing brought freshness and zest to one's senses. Birds were flying hither and thither from fruit-laden trees. A strange yearning was awakened in one's heart, simply by listening to their chirping and warbling. Peacocks were dancing colourfully everywhere. It was a season for enjoyment. I was surrounded by the women of my household. An atmosphere of singing and dancing pervaded the air. I was being fanned by adorned ladies, with fans made of peacock feathers. Every individual was affected by a strange atmosphere of banter and passion:

Paradise is where there is no pain
And everyone minds his own business

All of a sudden, my younger brother, *Jarnail*[30] Mirza Sikandar Hashmat Bahadur, joined the merry-making. After a while, he informed me that he had selected a woman for performing *mujra*[31] – who in addition to being exceedingly beautiful, was well versed in singing and dancing too. I replied, "It would have been proper had you presented her to me." Seeing my impatience for meeting a stranger, he explained that having danced and sung for a long time, she was extremely tired, but I should be patient, as she would be brought in my presence in due course of time.

Because I had no alternative, I had to control the eagerness in my heart. But I started feeling the pangs of separation from her. The very next day, when the merry-making commenced again, my younger brother, *Jarnail* Saheb Mirza Sikandar Hashmat Bahadur made his presence. With him was a young woman, whose visage glittered like a gemstone. Her graceful walk created a yearning in one's heart. Laughing and joking with her companions, she was coming forward smilingly and playfully, with a certain unique charm. She would be around eighteen years of age. Her name was Waziran, and she was the daughter of a *tawa'if*[32] by the name of Bi Jan, who lived near Kasab bridge. The moment we looked into each others' eyes, the arrow of love pierced my heart. Realising that the ongoing festivities were for those of equal status, I chose to remain silent, quietly bearing the turmoil within me, although I was swept away by my emotions. I would have professed my love for her, but I chose to control myself and was in a state of self-mortification, when Waziran started her song and dance:

Was beauty not enough that one had to open the mirror itself..
One more surprise for those who were already surprised.

There, she was engrossed in her performance, and here, I was watching her with tears of emotion. Eventually, I could no longer find the strength to control my senses, and ordered that the assembly be dispersed.

The next day, she again cast such a spell on the audience with her charms and mesmerized me to such an extent that I could no longer eat, drink or sleep properly. Her eyes so hypnotized me that I was fluttering like a cock bird who was being slaughtered. In those days, a woman named Najm un-Nisa Begum was employed in my household on security duty. About forty – forty five years of age, she was an aunt of my wife, *Khas Mahal* and also related to me by way of my in-law, Ali Nafaq Mohammad Ali Khan Madar-ud-Daula. She was an efficient, understanding and cultured woman, who was extremely devoted to me. She understood me so well that she could anticipate my wish and carry it out, before I had even expressed myself. An extremely good natured and well dressed woman, she was the custodian of my money and for her, my satisfaction was of prime concern, instead of her own comfort. Well proportioned and physically attractive for her age, she was a witty and intelligent woman. In her family, she was known as Pyare Saheb. When she was appointed on guard duty in my household, she was given the title of *daroga* Najm un-Nisa Begum. She would be in my vicinity day and night and, from the expression in my eyes, understand what was going on in my heart. *Daroga* Najm un-Nisan Begum had appointed eighteen other women, each with an individual talent, style and grace. If it can be said that each was unique in her own way, it would not be an exaggeration.

In short, when *daroga* Najm un-Nisan Begum noticed that my life was in peril (!), and I was fast losing my patience, one day she fell at my feet and cried, "O *Jān-é-Alam*, my life is at your disposal! After all, what matters so much to you, that you have no concern even for your own life? Why is the flame of happiness of a good man getting extinguished like this by the draught of sadness? By the grace of Allah, the heavens may fall, but this servant of yours will not shirk from her duty towards you."

In those days, Mir Mohammad Mehdi was working as *daroga* in my household. He was related to the family of Amin-ud-Daula Hussain Khan, who had been *Wazir*[34] during the reign of my late father. He had also been my mentor. I had learnt mathematics and economics from him. Mir Mohammad Mehdi was a *Sayyid*[35]. He was the commander of a military battalion on a monthly salary of Rs 15 per month. He was a holy and good natured person but with a proud nature. Due to this reason, he had been removed from his post. He was educated, around thirty two years of age, fair complexioned and of average build. Through the good offices of Amin-ud-Daula Imdad Hussain Khan, Mir Mohammad Mehdi had secured employment in my government as *daroga,* because in those days, Nawab Amin-ud-Daula wielded considerable influence. But somehow, I could not come to terms with this new *daroga*. This was the reason others interfered in his work also. He too felt that I should forget my prejudices and accept him. Consequently, he sought to derive advantage from the present situation, by trying to help me out in this impasse (with Waziran). One day, he exclaimed, "O *Jān-é-Alam*! What was the reason behind your sadness and impatience and also, all enjoyment and merry making had come to an end." In those days, two female singers were presented before me. One was named Amman and the other Imaman. Before coming to my court, they had achieved fame in the households of the rich in Farrukhabad. God knows why they chose to leave all that and approach my court, where they were awarded with the title, *Surur-e-Mehfil Waliyan*. They were actually sisters by relation, whose mother was named Majju and father was called Nathu. Their brothers were Ghulam Raza and Gehman, but addressed as Chacha Ghulam Nabi and Mamu Ghulam Haider. They will be discussed later. For the benefit of the reader, only their names are being mentioned as of now.

Amman and Imaman truly loved me. Together with *daroga* Najm un-Nisan, they would take care of all my needs. I accepted Amman and Imaman as my sisters. These three women had a special place in my heart, and I did not take any decision without first consulting them. Of course, I would be suffering in the throes of love for Waziran. Whenever my senses would be inflamed in the desire for that precious flower from the garden of beauty, these three of my close friends and confidants would soothe me by singing romantic songs. In those days only, I started composing *thumris*[36] as a passion.

Gradually, these three women, through their dedication and close proximity to me, came to know about my secret love. And in the court, *daroga* Mir Mohammad Mehdi would try to enquire about my condition through diverse methods. One day, *daroga* Najm un-Nisan Begum went to Bi Jaan's home. In a subtle manner, she probed Waziran's inner emotions, and realised that Waziran too was deeply in love with me. Her feet were shackled in her love for me, due to which she would sigh loudly. When Najm un-Nisan reached there, Waziran conveyed her feelings to her in a very agitated and restless manner. Najm un-Nisan also noticed that Waziran's mother was sitting close by, like a baleful tigress. She would not let Waziran speak openly. Due to this, *daroga* Najm un-Nisan returned disappointed, without achieving anything.

Here, I was lying in bed, helpless, feeling extremely distressed, as if surrounded by a season of sorrow and regret. My eyes would be clouded over, and I would sigh heart-rendingly, like a fish out of water remembering a river. Seeing this condition of mine, *daroga* Najm un-Nisan, Amman and Imaman fell at my feet and stated that I should not be sighing like this. Had I not heard of this couplet:

"There is no problem that cannot be solved
A man should not be afraid (he should be fearless)

God willing, we will present that beauteous fairy to you. Please give us some time. Till that moment, *huzoor*[37] should be patient and take things easy, lest Waziran's mother petition before your father and the work at hand be spoiled."

I remained in bed in agony, lovelorn and helpless. My health was steadily deteriorating, and whenever I found myself increasingly disconcerted, I would play the *sitar* or sing painfully romantic songs, trying to soothe my heart's desires. Food became an anathema for me. These three women felt that this fatal beauty should be in my possession, on some pretext or the other. However, because the mother was an exceedingly cunning woman, their plans could not materialise. On another occasion, *daroga* Najm un-Nisan visited Waziran's home, and found her lying on a cot, crying her eyes out. Najm un-Nisan, by way of gestures tried to inform Waziran about my infatuation for her. But suddenly, the heartless mother appeared and spoke, "What is the purpose of a government official's visit to the house of a prostitute? We have nothing to do with you. Please do not come here, else we will approach the court and petition the king!"

On hearing this, *daroga* Najm un-Nisan left the house in haste, and came to me in a helpless manner. I observed that she was trembling with irritation and self-mortification, having a disappointed look on her face. When I asked for the reason for this, she narrated how the mother had threatened to create a ruckus over the issue. After hearing the entire episode, I was immensely angered and immediately informed Mir Mohammad Mehdi that I would not touch food or water unless my sweetheart came to me. It was also possible that I would give up my life this way and then he would be regretful; because of all this, he should stake his life on bringing her (Waziran) to me.

For some time, he was thoughtful. Then he hazarded that although fetching her was not a difficult task, how long could this be kept as a secret from my royal father. During all this, a month passed, but my desires could not be fulfilled. In this connection, I also sent word to Amin-ud-Daula, and few other women employed in my father's household, *viz.* Musa Hibul Sultan and Intezam Sultan were also put on the job, but there was no success and I continued in my lovelorn state.

One day, I climbed on the roof of *Badshah Manzil* (my house) with a pistol in my hand and locked the door from inside. I wanted to blow my head off, but *daroga* Najm-un-Nisan started hitting the door with her head, exclaiming, "O *Jān-é-Alam*! I beseech you in the name of the Almighty – just listen to me." I replied from inside, "What do you want to say?" She replied, "Just give me one more chance. If this time, I do not bring her to you, you can do whatever you wish. Now that your desires are on the verge of fulfilment, what is the point of hurting yourself?" I heeded to her plea and controlled myself. At that very moment, Sheikh Ghulam Ali rode fast on his horse, to Waziran's home. I had my home decorated – a nuptial bed was arranged in the middle of the stream, which had fountains on either side. Other than Mir Mohammad Mehdi, there was no one nearby, like the couplet:

As the time of union of lovers finally approaches
The flames of my desires flare up..

Happiness and excitement made me impatient. Then I saw that beauty lighting up my house like the moon. I rushed to her and took her in my lap. Like a moth caught in a flame, I was consumed in the fire of my passion for her beauty. The night was spent in mutual remonstrance and exchanging lovers' complaints and secrets. The next day dawned with the cock's crowing and morning call of *Allahu Akbar*. With that, my soul, which had soared in the ecstasy of our union, became like a bird sacrificed. From behind the door, the voice of Mir Mohammad Mehdi cautioned me, "Morning has broken, *huzoor*. It would be proper if you now bid farewell." This warning of Mir's made me panic and my patience also gave way. In this condition, I bid her Godspeed (farewell). For a whole month, a somewhat similar situation prevailed. One day, I controlled myself and honoured Amin-ud-Daula with robes and titles, for his unwavering loyalty and services provided to me[38].

Another Incident of that Fatal Beauty

One day she was in her home, near Kasab bridge, which I have mentioned earlier. She was suffering from high fever, due to which her eyes were half-closed. And here I was, suffering from the pangs of desire for her. The moment I thought of her, what I saw was that she was standing near me, in her feverish condition. She was bare-foot, wrapped in a white sheet only. She had come to me in this very condition, after covering a distance of about one *kos*[39] on foot. I asked her, "What was the need to come here in this condition?" She replied, "Maybe I remembered my heart (love)" and collapsed in a faint. It is worth pondering upon – that such incidents were described in old stories, but here I was, seeing it with my own eyes.

Festivities and merry-making marked the day my beloved entered my house and sat beside me. Singers with dulcet tones and beauty comparable to angels made the gathering an object of envy for the heavens. Greetings and blessings rent the air from every side, echoing sweetly in the breeze. On this occasion of happiness, I arranged for a feast in honour of Hazrat Ali[40]. Gifts were given to retainers, each one honoured as per their status in the court. Especially *daroga* Najm un-Nisan Begum, Amman and Imaman. The mother of Waziran had been jailed on the orders of Amin-ud-Daula. After a few months, she was released from prison under my direction. From her daughter's side, she was given a sum of rupees two thousand, and honoured with a shawl and handkerchief. I had wanted that she should reside with her daughter, but she did not wish to quit her illicit livelihood and stay with her daughter. As a result of this, the object of my desire, Waziran, was most annoyed with her mother.

Waziran was provided with the most precious jewels, silverware and utensils of gold, faithful attendants and honorific titles. Her last title was Mallika-e-Alam Nawab Nigar Mahal. For a year, she was like a star on the ascendant. After this, due to certain reasons, her fortunes declined. She became so careless by nature that in the daytime, she could not recall any matter conveyed to her in the previous night. I had not intended that she should mingle with my other *begums*, but she did not pay heed and became friendly with the rest of them. This attitude of hers pained me deeply. I had desired that no one should be at par with Nigar Mahal in status. But she could not differentiate between friend and foe, confidante and stranger. Neither did she make any effort to pay heed to me in this regard. Against my wishes, she became friends with Umda Begum, Nishat Mahal and Nanhi Begum. In fact, I had wanted that Nigar Mahal to have a higher status than these *begums*. But when she started mingling with them, then where was the difference in status among them all. Other than this, some more issues emerged. Flippant attitude, not waiting to take our meals together, regarding love as a game of children and other myriad reasons gave cause for this unpleasant state of affairs.

Huzur-e-walia

The memoir of that queen of beauty concludes, and now I begin another. When that coquettish lover of mine behaved in an unfair manner towards me, my heart turned away from her and eventually, the intrigues of my enemies could succeed in this direction. I was twenty two years of age. At that time, through *daroga* Najm un-Nisan Begum, eighteen armed female guards were appointed[41]. By their dutiful services, they surpassed everyone else, and as a result, they were given the title of *Huzur-e-walia.* In a span of two years, through various ploys, I managed to romance all of them. But the conduct of these women was very inappropriate. Whatever they earned, they would recklessly spend on others, and amazingly, would declare themselves as my companions and confidantes. In those days, two eunuchs, named Bashir and Feroz, had been provided to me as *khwajasārās*[42], by my (late) father. I gave the charge of the store to Feroz and put Bashir on guard duty. Both were negroes; Bashir was fifty years of age and Feroz was forty years old. Both were brave and capable. Bashir was experienced and intelligent, although envious by nature. Feroz was short tempered and he was also illiterate.

When both settled down in their respective duties, Bashir started competing with Mir Mohammad Mehdi in devotion and loyalty, but he could not succeed. He also harboured malice against *daroga* Najm un-Nisan Begum. As a result of all this, he could not lead a peaceful life. But gradually, he did succeed in his designs. When Bashir came to know that I was romantically involved with the *huzur-e-walia*, he started behaving strangely; sometimes he would praise their comeliness and elegance and sometimes he would try to scare me by branding them unfaithful. Because this female platoon had been raised by *daroga* Najm un-Nisan Begum, Bashir, out of envy, wanted to usurp guard duty for himself, both outside and inside the palace premises.

Bashir was the same person, who had not only worked under (late) Nasir-ud-Din Haider, and Vilayati Mahal, he had also served in the court of my (late) grandfather, Mohammad Ali Shah, his queen, Malka-e-Jahan on security duty. Afterwards, my father affectionately presented Bashir to me. Keeping in view his antecedents, I made him look after the welfare of my *begums*. One evening, an entertainment programme of the court was in full swing, with my mind completely occupied with the passion for the *huzur-e-walia*, with each one exhibiting her beauty and coquetry. During the programme, a *huzur-e-wali,* Haidri Khanum, requested that she may be allowed to leave the gathering and go home. Bashir exclaimed, "Lord! She is deceiving you. Whatever wealth, jewellery and ornaments she gets from you, she showers on her admirers outside. For how long will this act of charity go on? Whoever remains in your service, as desired by *daroga* Najm un-Nisan, should definitely be honoured and have her head held high, but what is the point in honouring those who obtain everything from here, but choose to squander it outside? And moreover, this woman is neither beautiful nor good natured."

On hearing his speech, I replied, "These women are ready to sacrifice their lives for me. If I only give a sign, they can cut off their heads and present it to me. The *Huma* bird[43] cannot be benefited by associating with a crow. And neither can the *Huma* bird be at a loss, if the crow lives with it." Bashir retorted, "My lord, because of the beauty and comeliness of these women, you are unaware of their treachery…." Cutting short his diatribe, I replied, "Your opinion is not correct. I will ask them to reside here."

When I asked the *huzur-e-walis* to reside here (in the palace), they immediately dilly-dallied, raising objections and excuses. So evidently Bashir's complaints had some weight. One of the women said, " How can I leave my ancestral house?" Another stated, "I have children. How can I remain here." Although one did assure me, "I am ready to serve here day and night." The situation collapsed like a house of cards. I was much pained on observing their treachery.

Sadly, out of eighteen women, not one had any regard for me or my affection for them. At that very moment, I was repelled by that congregation and came to the conclusion that the solicitude of uncaring, indifferent women was akin to harbouring serpents as pets, and it would be wholly proper if I sidelined myself from them. Consequently, all of them were dismissed from my service. Their group dispersed like leaves scattered in the sand by the autumnal wind. Few of them did remain behind, but I did not pay any heed to their presence. They also asked to be pardoned, but I didn't listen to any of their prayers and excuses.

In short, the whole establishment now resembled a defunct workplace. But the love for a few of the *huzur-e-wali* did leave behind scars on my heart.

Qutub Ali Khan Sitar[44] Nawaz

Qutub Ali Khan was a famous *sitar* player of those times. He had been earlier employed by Mukhtar-ud-Daula Ibn Nasir-ud-Daula (late)[45] for playing the *sitar*. Hailing from a Rajput family of Bareilly, he was also related to Raja Jagat Dev. Around thirty years of age, having a wheatish complexion, prominent moustaches, and a head-full-of hair, he was well educated, a prolific writer and also well versed in *shayari*[46] and music. In fact, it would be appropriate to say that being so accomplished in these fine arts, he was the Baiju, Gopal and Tansen of those times. To drive away my sorrows, I appointed him as my *ustad*[48], and I learnt the art (of playing sitar) so well, that people would be spell-bound when I played in gatherings. People would laugh with tears in their eyes. Pyare Khan would praise me and my *ustad* would also sway in appreciation. Sometimes, Qutub Khan would himself kiss my hands.

I took this talent to dizzying heights. From that moment onwards, Qutub Khan became my close friend and confidante.

But he was an atheist. Daily, he would spend six to twelve hours in my company. One day, he brought a message for meeting Taj Mahal, who was the wife of (late) Nasir-ud-Din Haider. She had conveyed her desire, through one of her female attendants also. But keeping the dignity and respect for my uncle in mind, I replied to the contrary. Qutub Ali Khan was also amorous in nature. He had many facets in his personality, including the mastery of several Arabic languages, sensibility and a humorous nature.

A month had elapsed since my last encounter with the *huzur-e-wali*. I started thinking about how long I could tolerate this hurting of desire and disappointment. It would be better if I summoned a few of my lovers, so I would forget the *huzur-e-wali.*

Yasmin Pari

After a lot of searching and efforts, a woman could be ultimately identified, who was given the title, Yasmin Pari[49]. I tried my level best to entangle her in a web of love, but due to her nonchalant nature, I could not succeed.

Suleiman Pari

Only a few days had passed, when I introduced another woman in my household and gave her the title, Suleiman Pari.

Izzat Pari

After some time, I came in contact with another woman. Because she herself had expressed her desire to join my establishment, I gladly agreed. At that very moment, I brought her home, gave her the title of Izzat Pari and introducing her to Mahrukh Pari[50] (see later) asked the latter, if she knew the former. She replied in the affirmative and requested that she be allowed to talk to Izzat Pari alone. In short, in the name of Mahrukh, I paid rupees five hundred to her mother, who happily signed her consent and contentedly went home. By the grace of God, I had never met such a good-natured woman before in my life.

Sultan Pari

Two dancing girls by the name of Haidri and Dilbar enjoyed an outstanding reputation in Lucknow for their singing and dancing skills. Dilbar, who was the elder sister, had performed for me and was obliged to me. Therefore, she presented her younger sister as a tribute to me. Haidri was eleven years old at that time. She had a fleeting knowledge of song and dance. I accepted Dilbar's tribute and gave the title of Sultan Pari to Haidri. Thus, I obtained Yasmin Pari through *khwajasara* Bashir, Sultan Pari through Mir Akbar Ali, Izzat Pari through the efforts of *Khas Mahal* (Alam Ara Begum), and this girl (Haidri) through the offices of *daroga* Najm un-Nisan Begum.

Hur Pari

Hardly any time had passed when this girl (Haidri) had come, that a woman by the name of Najja, came to me through *daroga* Mir Mehdi. I gave her the title of Hur Pari. She was the daughter of Amiran *domni*[51], who had taken to prostitution as a means of livelihood.

Mahrukh Pari[50]

After this, *daroga* Manoranj sent Mehboob, a prostitute[52] to me, through coercion and some other means. She was adept in dancing and playing the *sarod*[81] with her fame having spread far and wide. Ironically, in every age, the role of the *daroga* (policeman) is somewhat like this only. I cannot say how they will justify their actions before God. When they observed that the crown prince of Awadh kingdom had given general orders for presenting singing and dancing girls to him, they did not hesitate to force women to present themselves for my pleasure. Anyway, in this way, a woman was brought in my presence. When I examined her condition, and invited her to join my household, she flatly refused my offer and informed me that she had been deceived into coming. When I saw that neither was she interested in staying at my home, nor did she have any regard for me, I replied that she could happily return to her home. The Lord above would surely provide other women for me. On hearing me, she responded, "*Jān-é-Alam*! With all due respect to you, how can I leave now and go away. I hope that your goodself will include me in your harem of *paris* (fairies) so my self esteem will also be benefited."

Her request was accepted and she was given the title, Mahrukh Pari. One day, while I was on my way, a female relative of hers blocked my path, by prostrating herself in front of the horses of my carriage. This was during the times when I used to pay daily respects to my father, and was on my way to do so. I was very much perturbed by that woman's lamentations, and asked her who she was and what she wanted. At this, she replied, "*Daroga* Tafreeh has abducted my daughter and presented her to you. I want justice from you." Immediately I brought that woman home, and asked Mahrukh Pari about her. She replied in the affirmative, and asked to be allowed to talk to her in private. In the name of Mahrukh, I gave rupees five hundred to her mother, who readily signed the agreement and happily went back to her home. By the grace of Allah, I had never come across such a good natured woman.

Noor Afshahan Pari

Through the magnanimity of *Khas Mahal* (Alam Ara Begum), a woman entered my harem, who was given the title of Noor Afshahan Pari. Later, with my permission, she proceeded on a pilgrimage to *Karbala*.

The Courtesan Waziran

During this period, a courtesan named Waziran started expressing her love for me. This was the same Waziran, who has been mentioned in the previous pages, and who was initially in the court of Nasir-ud-Din Haider as a court singer. And who was now dependent on Shaidi Haider. Not only me, this woman had captivated several others, with her wheatish complexion, well proportioned limbs and attractive eyes. She was around thirty years old. Lively, flirtatious and playful by nature. Initially, my younger brother, Mirza Sikandar Hashmat was entangled in her charms. Subsequently, she managed to swindle him out of thousands of rupees. She would also act playful and coquettish with me. Sometimes, she would send me romantic messages through *daroga* Najm un-Nisan Begum. Her prolific messages would be signed in her own blood. An example of her devotion towards me was that to just have a look at me, she would go to the *dargah*[53] of Hazrat Abbas, just, on the same days when I would be visiting the shrine. Because I was already aware of her involvement with my brother, Hashmat, one day, I said, "On one side, you are romantically involved with my brother, and on the other hand, you are also trying to link with me. After all, how is it possible to desire two men at a time?" At this, she apologized and declared that she did not have any attachment with my brother whatsoever.

One day, a musical soirée was in progress. The moon cast its gentle light everywhere. The melodious voices of singers had the audience spell bound, piercing their hearts. From the decorations, it appeared that instead of a night of entertainment, it was the wedding night of a young bride. Through the efforts of gardeners, the premises had been converted into a heavenly garden, by strategically placing bouquets and flowers. My friends and acquaintances were seated around me, joking and laughing. In this gathering, by coincidence, my younger brother, Mirza Sikandar Hashmat Bahadur was also present. I enquired of him, "I hear that you are in a relationship with Waziran. Or is it just a rumour?" At this, my brother replied, "She frequently sends me her declarations of love through my courtiers. I still have her letters with me." On hearing this from my brother, I responded that this woman had sent me similar overtures. My brother and I noted that through a coincidence, this gathering had several respectable people present and if she indicated her preference in their midst, her submission would be considered as final. And we brothers would henceforth have no grievances against each other in future. In short, that adept dancer, while performing a dance, moved forward and held my hand. And she stated that she had no relations with Sikandar Mirza Hashmat – she did not even know who he was.

This declaration of hers caused the gathering to rejoice, with song and music bursting forth with happiness. But my brother was mortified at this conduct of a mere prostitute, and left the gathering[54]. I also ordered that the gathering be dispersed. After this incident, my relations with Waziran progressed rapidly. Other than these interests, I was also keen on drama and plays. Accordingly, we decided mutually that on a particular day, I would visit Azimullah Naib Kaptan and she promised that she too would reach the place as decided.

Without doubt, it was clear that there was no bar for her entering my household. But all this was being done so that the fire of passion for me would be more intense in her heart, and make her impatient to meet me.

Ali Naqi Khan and Waziran

Eventually, that day arrived and I started making preparations to visit Azimullah's house. Side by side, I made arrangements for a cultural programme for my companions and attendants – who were freed from their duties for the day, and also put guards in the doorways, so that to-and-fro movement would be restricted. After getting free from all these arrangements, I put on a formal, silken dress embossed with the royal crown, and a golden turban. Astride my mount, I reached the house of Azimullah. I was accompanied by *daroga* Najm un-Nisan Begum and two torch bearers. Azimullah was around fifty years of age, a Sheikh by descent, but somewhat quirky in nature. The moment he saw me, he stood up, paid his courtesies and provided me with a chair to sit on. He then presented *paan* and *itr*[55] to me, which I accepted. Ali Naqi Khan, my father-in-law by relation, was also present on the occasion. He was the son of late Madar-ud-Daula, and a Sayyid by descent. Tall, mustachioed and slim, he was an extremely intelligent, polished and suave gentleman, he would be around forty years old. He was used to a life of luxury and opulence. On seeing me, he immediately stood up as a mark of respect.

I moved forward and sat beside him. After all these formalities were over, I noticed that the arrangements were limited and my beloved, with eyes that could kill, was not present. I enquired of Azimullah about her whereabouts, to which he replied that she would be present shortly. Till such time, the melodies of the sitar provided a magnificent backdrop. After a few moments, that graceful beauty also made her presence. We embraced, but she was in a strange condition; sometimes she would weep and then again, sometimes break into peels of laughter.

It was the rainy season and the sky was overcast with dark clouds. I feared that if it started to rain, I would not be able to return home. On a note of regret, tinged with extreme desire, I bid her farewell. That day, I had met Ali Naqi Khan for the first time. On reaching home, I saw that the cultural gathering was in full sway. I went straight to bed, where I lay down. Because the night was almost over, I fell asleep. *Daroga* Najm un-Nisan Begum also went to sleep in her bedroom. In short, the magic of my love had affected Waziran too. And here I was, wounded by the arrows of her coquetry. Sometimes she would wound me and sometimes I would wound her.

Training of the *Paris*

I could not ignore the fact that new performers needed to be identified and encouraged. Because of this reason, there was a constant search, for those having musical talents, so that the training of the *paris* could continue uninterrupted, and they could become adept in the art. Amman and Imaman informed me one day that few relatives of theirs had acquired great proficiency in the performing arts. On hearing this, I ordered Amman and Imaman to present them before me. On the fourteenth day of the moon (almost full moon), to wait for them, I myself settled down beneath the dome of the main palace, sitar in hand, but hidden behind veiled curtains and accompanied by Amman and Imaman. After some time, four people entered. One was the father of the sisters. He was called Nathu Khan. The second one was a paternal uncle. His name was Ghulam Ali. The third was Gehman Jaan, a brother in relation, and the fourth was Ghulam Haider, their maternal uncle. These four immediately started playing the *sarod* after a dance number, and here, I too was playing the sitar, from behind the curtains. That moment was so magical that the very walls and doorways, the moon and the stars appeared to be wonder-struck. Words of praise were spoken by all present in the gathering. Their performance was so effective that I lowered my head behind the veiled curtains.

After that day, Nathu Khan and Gehman Jaan were appointed as teachers for Hur Pari and Sultan Pari. Other than these, many others accomplished in the art of song and dance were given jobs. Sabit Ali and Chajju Khan were appointed to train other *paris*, and every day, a cultural gathering would be organised for entertainment and enjoyment. I, myself, would practice with other students of Nathu Khan, and after sometime, I became such an adept that I left my teacher far behind. Ghulam Raza used to be in my employ in those days. I have already discussed him previously. He was of short height with broad forehead and large eyes - respectful and carefree by nature. He also possessed tremendous physical strength. One day, he broke the antlers of a deer into splinters. He was also very faithful. For all these reasons, I ordered him to be present near me all the time.

Decoration of *Parikhana*

I reserved a small house for educating *paris* in music and song. It was decorated with a lot of thought and became a *PARIKHANA*[56] – a challenge for the heavens themselves. White marble flooring was laid, which was decorated with beautiful porcelain vases. Expensive cots and beds were arranged in profusion. The entrance was guarded by Turkish female guards, who prevented unauthorised entry of strangers. Of course, *daroga* Najm un-Nisan Begum, Amman and Immam had complete unhindered access to the place.

Ghulam Raza, Gehman Jaan, Chajju Khan and Sabit Ali would be present in the *Parikhana* for most of the day, and due to their presence, the festive atmosphere remained live. And in this way, the *paris* would also be trained and tutored. I would also be totally engrossed in acquiring musical skills all day long.

A Meeting with Munna

My preoccupation with music and dance intensified with time. I desired that more women should be inducted for singing and dancing – the more, the better. I conveyed my desire to all and sundry. A new term, *ma'aruza* was coined for whosoever presented a singing and dancing woman in the court. For example, if a woman was presented through someone – it would be described as a *ma'aruza* being presented. It would indicate that the woman was to enter my household. In future, if the word, *ma'aruza* was used anywhere, it would denote the meaning given by me to it.

Once it so happened that *daroga* Najm un-Nisan Begum, Amman and Imaman stated in one voice that a *ma'aruza* had been arranged, who was unparalleled in beauty – so felt her admirers. So much so that even God may not have seen such a beauty. She was an expert *sarod* player and was blessed with many other talents also. She would be seventeen – eighteen years of age and this epitome of beauty had once seen me somewhere, and from that day onwards, food and drink became anathema to her. It was her heart's desire that she should be admitted to the group of *paris*. Her name was Munna. When I enquired about her antecedents, I came to know that she was the niece of Waziran, and she had kept it hidden from her aunt that she desired to serve me. On hearing this, I lost my self-control. In my eagerness to meet her, I spent many restless days and sleepless nights. With time, this state-of-affairs reached Waziran. This agitated her so-much-so that her life became a burden for her. She started burning up in this love triangle. Through various subtle ways, she tried to draw me away from Munna. Conversely, my desire for her became even more intense. Eventually, through the efforts of the three women (*daroga* Najm un-Nisan Begum, Amman and Imaman), Munna came to me one night. I cannot describe how I spent that night in pleasure and delight. As a punishment for her "offence", her community ostracized her and put her behind bars. But even during imprisonment, she could not free herself from my memories – and in jail, sometimes she would weep, sometimes enquire about my welfare. Eventually, due to the efforts of Mir Mehdi, she was freed and she joined my household.

My love for her completely engulfed my heart. She also observed the beautiful *paris* and lovers of my household, and their musical skills in cultural gatherings, which made her increasingly envious and jealous. She started thinking of ways and means to subdue her raging emotions. When Munna entered my household, Waziran stopped meeting me and initiated intimacy with Hakim Nawab Mirza and Ali Baksh Risaldar. After some time, she moved away from them and ensnared Shaidi Ahmad, who was the brother of Haji Khanum. Nowadays, full of deprivation, she is leading a troubled life at his home. I have already mentioned Shaidi Ahmed. He was around fifty years of age. God knows why she is lying around with that old, decrepit man. *Lā hawla wa lā quwwat*[57]*!!*

The Treachery of Munna

During this time, a *tabla*[58] player by the name of Chote Khan came to Lucknow. He originally belonged to Shahjahanabad. An adept at playing the instrument, he was destined to attain great heights with his skill. As he had come in search of a livelihood, he tried to get a job in my establishment. In due course, he was included in the group of *tabla* players under the care of Sheikh Ghulam Ali. He was about thirty five years old, with an attractive and muscular personality. Professional women (= prostitutes) would very often swoon over him. He also knew how to respond appropriately. In fact, he was a master of unusual talents. To call him a professional loverboy would not be out of place. Due to these talents, he came to my notice, and benefited from them also. Gradually, with his co-players, he also earned the sobriquet of *Bahar-e-Mehfil*[59]. Moreover, he became so close to me that he attained the status of Ghulam Murtaza. He had some weakness for Imtiaz.

Munna or Imtiyaz Pari continued to be consumed by the agony of enviousness for no good reason. One day, in a fit of unreasonable passion and rage, she decided to return to her home, but I did not allow her to do so. At this, she said that at the most, she wanted to go for an hour or so and I would not have to wait long for her. I was caught in her deceit and permitted her to proceed. But when she did not return for two days, I was very worried and deputed *daroga* Najm un-Nisan Begum to her house. But she refused to return and did not agree to come back at any cost. I was very much hurt by this conduct of hers, and I could do no more than grit my teeth.

Demise of Imtiaz Pari

Through Feroz, a *khwajasārā*, I came across another eunuch slave by the name of Mohammad Hussain. This person had been previously in the service of the wife of Saifullah Mir Hadi. He was a twenty five years old youth, with an extremely gentle, honest and sacrificing demeanour. He had no vices, and he obliged me in some matters, so much so that I am still in his debt. He was always alert and willing to provide his services. When I came to know about Imtiaz Pari through *daroga* Najm un-Nisan Begum, I was beside myself in rage, and commanded Mohammad Hussain Khan *khwajasara* to immediately bring her to me, by dragging her, if necessary. On hearing this order, Mohammad Hussain Khan, without hesitation, went forth, and after sometime, I saw that he had brought Imtiaz Pari by dragging her. She was weeping inconsolably, but still she did not pay heed to my order. When she was brought before me, I spat on her face and asked if was this the face by which she used to profess her love for me?

In short, I kept her in my establishment for a few days[60], but I could feel that she had developed inimical feelings for me, and wanted to go back to her home at any cost. I presented her with a diamond ring and bid her farewell. After this, I never thought of calling her back. A year passed by after this incident - when I was informed that Munna had died of tuberculosis.

Dilruba Pari

After being rid of Imtiaz Pari, I was passing my time in leisure with the other *paris*, immersed in their song and dance. Days were like *Eid*[61] and nights like *Shab-e-Barat*[62]. One day, through the good offices of Akbar-ud-Daula Bahadur, a courtesan by the name of Chunni came to my court to perform *mujra*. The moment I set my eyes on her, I became enamoured with her. She took off her ornaments and gave them to her mother, Faiju, and announced that she would not leave the court now. The mother started weeping and crying. At this, Chunni presented Faiju with two thousand rupees, and bid her goodbye. Faiju was beside herself in joy, and she immediately signed the consent papers, letting Chunni to remain behind in the court, after which she went home[63]. I gave the title of Dilruba Pari to Chunni.

Court spies conveyed this incident to the notice of my father, who summoned Dilruba Pari in this presence. On hearing this, I was much troubled at the thought of parting from her. Dilruba consoled me by saying, "*Huzoor*, please don't be saddened like this. Send me (to your father) fearlessly. I shall show him the written consent given by my mother, to convince him that I have not come here through forceful means or coercion." Although her approach was logical, I did not feel like parting from her. But I had no choice over the matter.

Accompanied by Mir Mohammad Mehdi, I unwillingly sent her to my father. On presenting herself there, she immediately stated, "I am at the mercy of your Highness. I hate unlawful activities, and I want to lead a respectable life. As proof, I can show the written consent of my mother in this regard." The king replied, "Let the consent be presented." With bowed head, she presented the consent. After examining the document, it was ordered that this woman should be respectfully escorted to the palace of the *Wali Ahad Bahadur* (Wajid Ali Shah). In fact, my head is bowed down under the obligation of that woman. She might have been 30 years old. Wheatish complexion, broad forehead, sharp featured and an adept in song and dance. When she stayed behind with me, she spent a lot of time in training other *paris*. My love for her grew with the passage of time.

I had arranged for different attires for the *paris*, and the responsibility for this rested with *Khas Mahal* (Alam Ara Begum). To be honest, she went about discharging her responsibilities with great dedication and interest. Several lakhs of rupees were spent in this enterprise.

Sarfaraz Pari

She was a professional courtesan by the name of Ganna. But later, after giving up her profession and marriage to a relative as per *shariat*[64] law, she was leading a respectable life like other good women. It is said that once she saw me in a dream and was entranced in a frenzied sort of way. At that very moment, the arrows of love for me pierced her heart. She was about 27 years old, with a pock marked face, attractive eyes and well-proportioned body. She came in contact with Feroz *khwajasārā* through the guard, Sheikh Ghulam Ali, and she conveyed her desire to join my group of *paris*. I considered her request, but because her husband was around, I had some hesitation in keeping her in my household. Eventually, she divorced her husband in the witness of Hazrat Mujtahid-ul-Astr Qibla and after that, there was no dilemma from my side on keeping her with me. I gave her the elevated title of Sarfaraz Pari and compared to other *paris*, I was more engrossed in my love for her. She was indeed a very happy-go-lucky and fashionable woman.

Haidri Begum

Haidri Begum, who recited *marsiya,* was employed by me in those days. She was a gentle and chaste woman, whom I respected from the core of my heart. She had come to me through *daroga* Najm un-Nisan Begum and wished to be included as a *begum*, but I did not agree to her wish. In frustration, she consumed ground glass; when I came to know of this, fearing my father, I promptly relieved her from her services and sent her home.

Sardar Pari

A daughter of a courtesan, barely eleven years old, was presented to me by wont of Amman and Imaman. She was beautiful, fair and delicate, with attractive eyes. She wanted to be trained in music. She was given the title of Sardar Pari and provided the requisite training.

Ajaib Khanum

A woman was brought to me, through *Khas Mahal* (Alam Ara Begum), to whom I gave the title of Ajaib Khanum. She was highly proficient in singing and dancing.

Nauchandi of *Rajab*[65]

I arranged for sending all the *paris* to the *dargah* of Hazrat Abbas during the sighting of the new moon in the month of *Rajab.* Costly dresses and ornaments of great value were provided to them, in addition to delicately decorated palanquins. Their procession was a strange sight to behold. It is possible that even the heavens might not have seen such a sight. I sent *daroga* Mir Mohammad Mehdi and *daroga* Najm un-Nisan as escorts, along with the *paris.*

I came to know that the multitudes in the *bazaars* and also those present at the *Dargah Sharif* had their eyes glued on the procession. It also came to my notice that on that very night, having an eyeful by Haider Hussain Khan caused a minor altercation, which was controlled intelligently by Mir Mohammad Mehdi. After spending the night at the *dargah,* they returned safely the next morning, and were grateful to me for providing them with such an opportunity. But my father was very much angered when he came to know of this incident and he forbade such actions in the future. Actually, except for three women (whom I had accepted as *Mahal* and kept behind veil), all others did not find any meaning for the custom. I then realised that one cannot be forced to fall in love. For this, it is necessary that a lover should be set free, to gauge the depth of her feelings of love. And this was the reason due to which I considered it essential to send the *paris* to the *dargah*[66].

Suleiman Mahal

The days were passing by when one day, I was informed that Nawab Nishat Mahal and Suleiman Pari were expecting[67]. I was overjoyed at this news. Congratulations poured in from every corner. On hearing the news, I immediately put Suleiman Pari in confinement, and granted her the title of Suleiman Mahal. She was also provided with appropriate gifts, clothes, ornaments and utensils. By the Grace of God, on the date of delivery, the *mahals* gave birth to the Moon and Jupiter, whose radiance brightened up the world(!). Nawab Nishat Mahal had given birth to a prince, hence her mother was honoured with honorary accoutrements and nose ring and my son was given the title of Mirza Sipahr Qadr. Nawab Suleiman gave birth to a daughter. Her grandfather (Amjad Ali Shah) gave her the title of Sipahr Ara Kubra Begum. Praise be to Allah!!

Sipahr Ara

My sister, married to Sarfaraz-ud-Daula, the son of my uncle, Munir-ud-Daula, had no surviving children. My mother suggested to my father that my daughter, Sipahr Ara be adopted by them.

Sometimes, Sipahr Ara Begum would be brought to her mother to see. After spending a night with us, the next morning she would be taken back. I did not like all this and the child's parting troubled me. But it was the wish of my parents. What could I do? To fulfil their wish was my duty. It was an unspoken order for me.

Mirza Bedaar Bhakt

After a few days, I got the auspicious news that Nawab Khas Mahal was expecting. On hearing this, I offered the Friday prayers. After some time, she gave birth to a son as radiant as the moon. His grandfather presented the infant with a 11-gun salute. Kinsfolk and friends gave their congratulations and presents on the occasion. A celebration was held and a musical programme was organised. The *paris* wore beautiful clothes and adorned themselves with expensive ornaments. It was like an evening of *Eid.* It was a celebration which could not be paralleled ever. The child's grandfather gave him the title of Mirza Bedaar Bhakt. He was raised with a lot of love in the care of his elders.

Shams Ara Begum

Sometime later, the news was conveyed to me that the happiness was further in store, because an attendant of the household, Farkhanda Khanum was expecting. I offered thanksgiving prayers once again and put her behind the veil. But I did not confer the title of *mahal* to her[68]. Only the title of Farkhanda Khanum was granted to her. After the usual period of confinement, a daughter was born to her. Her grandfather gave her the honorific title of Shams Ara Begum.

Shahanshāh Pari

One day, a woman named Pyari came to me, through *daroga* (Stores) Feroz *khwajasārā* and Sheikh Hussain Ali. I ordered her to be included in the group of *paris*, gave her the title of Shahanshāh Pari and provided her with training in singing and dancing.

Mashuq Pari

Through the offices of Pyare Sahib Mohammad Hussain *khwajasārā*, a daughter of the Jahani *domni*, was brought to me. I liked her immensely and inducted her in my household. She was given the title of Mashuq Pari, and put to training in the art of song and dance.

Mehak Pari

Through Amman and Imaman, a professional courtesan who appealed to me, was included with the *paris* after being given the title of Mehak Pari[69]. Her training in music and dance commenced likewise.

Dildar Pari

Through Mohammad Hussain Ali *khwajasārā*, I came across a woman by the name of Bandi Jaan Ilahi. She was given the title of Dildar Pari. As per convention, her training in singing and dancing also commenced at the *Parikhana*.

Huzoor Pari

A girl by the name of Hussaini came to my notice through the good offices of *daroga* Najm un-Nisan Begum. I liked her but she only learnt a little of music. She was given the title of Huzoor Pari.

Mashuq-e-Khas

I will now relate a strange incident. When a musical gathering was being organised to celebrate the birth of Sipahr Qadr (son of Nishat Mahal), prominent singers and dancers had been invited for the occasion. A courtesan named *Achi* also joined the gathering. I was used to beautiful women, but I have no words to describe her loveliness, which was a wonder of nature - so one could not look away from her. Melodious voice, a gait like thunderbolts. A body which shone like silver, and accompanying coquetry. An extremely attractive, well-proportioned figure. Lips like flower petals. Attire like a garland of blooms. Someone who could compete with angels. She shattered the hearts of those in the audience through her gestures and coquettishness. It seemed that even the angels would forget to pray, after seeing her exquisiteness. Her laugh resembled a shower of flowers. At that time, I was seated in the balcony of *Gulzar Manzil*[70] and observing all this, was totally hypnotised by her elegance and charm.

In those days, I also possessed charm and good looks like any beautiful woman[71]. A magician would feel lost in the magic of my eyes. Yousuf, the angel, would find it difficult to compete with me. My tresses were curled, my eyes piercing – beauty and grace would bow before me. I was lively and playful – I could stop a running deer through a gesture of my eyes. I possessed a sharp chin, the weak could gather strength from my eyes. My lips were akin to magical herbs for lovers. My eyebrows were bow shaped and my forehead like the moon. My hair could entangle countless admirers and lovers would be smitten by a look from my eyes. My arms, like swords, could vanquish my lovers. I possessed tresses, dark like the night and cheeks rosy like the sunrise. My personality was so impressive that they could easily control the wiles of a thousand lovers.

In short, my object of desire would look upon me with desire and yearning. I too would be beside myself. Whenever she danced, she would come close to me and hold my hands, and I would tease her. Eventually the programme ended and she went home, but was wounded by the arrow of my love.

Some months passed by after this incident. During this period, there were occasions, twice or thrice, to meet her, but she was so scared of her mother that she never expressed her feelings for me openly. She kept her emotions bottled up inside her, which pained her considerably. She would start getting into frequent fights with her mother. In desperation, sometimes she would also send me messages. One day, I again invited her for a dance programme.

But immediately bid her goodbye, out of fear of my parents. This was because during this time, my parents had imposed certain restrictions on me. For this very reason, I never thought of including her in my establishment. However, through the efforts of Mir Akbar Ali, she finally came to me one day, after paying a compensation of rupees six thousand to her mother.

Yasmin Pari, who has been described by me previously, had acquired considerable prowess after undergoing prolonged training in the art of singing and dancing. Also, she had blossomed into an extremely beautiful woman. I always had a weakness for her, but due to her carefree, playful nature, and also ongoing training, I had not paid much attention to her. However, with the passage of time, she became a true fairy. I thanked the Almighty and expressed my desire to her. She was also equally enamored with me. Gradually, I became so infatuated with her that I could neither eat, drink or sleep properly. She would be busy with her singing and dancing and I would be immersed in her beauty and sensuousness. This continued for a year or so, as the star of her desire glittered high in the firmament of my thoughts. But then, due to certain issues, this passionate relationship broke apart. Actually, during that time, I was enraptured with Sarfaraz Pari, and Yasmin Pari could not tolerate this. The fire of envy consumed her. Because of this, I was left with no other option but to sever my relationship with her.

It was in those days only that through my close confidante, Ghulam Raza Khan[72], I appointed his brother Ghulam Haider Khan, and their relatives, Choté Khan, Ghaseeté Khan, Ghulam Ehsaan Khan, Mohammad Hasan Khan, Chajju Khan, Haider Ali, Nisar Ali, Qutub Ali, Khwaja Baksh Khan and gave them the title of *Musahebané Khurd*[73].

Mirza Faridun Qadr

Barely three months had passed in the training of Mashuq Pari, when I was informed about her pregnancy. I thanked the Lord

Almighty, immediately put her behind the veil and gave her the title of *mahal*. Costly dresses, jewellery and gifts were presented to her. Separate accommodation was also provided to her. After the usual period of confinement, on the ninth day of *Muharram*, a son was born to her. My father honoured the child with the title of Mirza Faridun Qadr Bahadur[74]. My status was also elevated, and simultaneously, Mashuq Pari was given the title of Mashuq Mahal.

Mehar Ara Begum

In those days, another heart gladdening news was conveyed to me that Izzat Pari was expecting. On hearing this news, thanksgiving prayers were offered and Izzat Pari was put behind the veil. She was conferred the title of Izzat Mahal, and was felicitated like other *begums*. In fact, both Mashuq Mahal and Izzat Mahal had become pregnant at the same time. Consequently on day 7 of *Muharram*, Izzat Mahal gave birth to a daughter, whose beauty spread illumination like the moon. She was given the title of Mehar Ara Begum. She was younger to her brother, Faridun Qadr Bahadur, by just two days.

Sad Demise of Najm un-Nisa Begum

I write this with a broken heart. I want to narrate something about Najm un-Nissa Begum. Because one should not, in moments of happiness, forget death. We are mere mortals, resembling bubbles in water. Every living being has to experience death one day. Intellectuals of this world regard this world as nothing but a form of water or to use a metaphor, a walking shadow. What we think as a shade, is soon overcome by harsh sunlight. Life and death are complimentary, correlated with each other. Consequently, after wiping my tears of sadness with the sleeve of hopelessness, I inform the reader that Najm un-Nisa Begum, *daroga* of the *zenana*[75], my friend and well-wisher, confidante, close companion, who doted on me and fluttered around me like a moth near the flame, died suddenly and left me floundering in agony and anguish.

When I heard this earth shattering news, stunned, I went to my bedroom, and cried my heart out. Other than this, what could I do? Helpless, I sat on my bed and prayed that she gets peace in death.

Amir Pari

A woman entered my household through Nawab Nishat Mahal. She was given the title of Amir Pari by me. Actually, she was a professional courtesan, famous by the name of Karambaksh Wali. Around 18 years of age, she was included with the *paris*, and put under training in music; because she was well-versed in the art, hence she did not have to make much effort. However, as she was prone to neglecting her talent due to carelessness, her training was continued so she would not lose her musical skills.

Wazir Pari

Feroz *khwajasārā* and Nawab Khas Mahal sent a woman to be considered by me. I liked her immensely and included her in my establishment. She was popularly known as Sukhbadan Wali. When, in the heat of summer, she displayed such a talent in singing and dancing, I accepted her without a second thought and gave her the title of Wazir Pari. Her training, too was continued.

Umrao and Umda Khanum

To relate a day's incident - singers were singing melodious songs, female attendants were engaged in coquettishly serving wine so much so that, one was destined to take leave of his good intentions. Singers and poets added a sweet richness to the milieu. The heady fragrance of flowers spread far and wide, assailing the senses. Flowery desires were being cast by the soft, gentle breeze as if by pick and choose. The royal palace was bedecked like a bride. Every lantern helped in visualising one's beloved in front of the eyes. Trees and bushes, decorated with rhinestones presented a fantastic sight. Portraits of former rulers and kings had been put up. An exquisite red carpet made of jute had been spread on the floor. Tall, tilting mirrors on frames, adorned the venue. Special arrangements had been made for the decoration and adornment of *Rāhat Manzil*. The stream of *Hazrat Bagh* presented an enchanting view for spectators. European-style lamps had been fitted with lampshades. Here and there, indiscreet gardeners tended to the bushes and trees. The pathways of the garden were exceedingly clean and clear. A fine table had been spread in the center of the palace grounds, on which European refreshments and dry fruits were being served in salvers made of glass, stone, gold and silver. Flower vases and priceless urns of different colours served as decorations. European forks and knives were available for spearing the chicken preparations kept in dishes. Recently appointed Mohd. Hussain Khan, a recently appointed *khwajasārā*[76] was the master of ceremonies of this function. The creations of *bawarchi*[77] Suhail (one star) graced the table like the moon surrounded by stars. Amphoras containing sherbets of lime and *phalsa*[78] were liberally available. All around the table, delicate and beautiful chairs had been kept for *paris*[49], as beauteous as flowers; the *paris* held forks and knives in their hands. A separate decorated seat, studded with precious gems had been provided for me. I too was adorned like a bridegroom. A coronet made of shining pearls rested on my head; I was dressed appropriately as per my status as crown prince. Strings of pearls encircled my neck and arms. My wrist bands were extravagantly priced. I wore red, satin pyjamas, adorned with pearls along the hems. My upper garments were also richly brocaded. I held a shining sword in my hand. My whole body was effused with the essence of *henna*[79]. My eyes were limpid with the languidness of youth. The playing of European musical instruments created an exquisite atmosphere. Beauteous *paris* were seductively singing melodiously and dancing before me. The occasion was the birthday celebration of the twelfth Imam[80] on the fifteenth day of *Shaban*[12]. I had spread the ringlets of my hair on my face that day.

All of a sudden, a lover and sweetheart, stylish and alluring appeared in front of me. It appeared that her eyes were impatient to kill with poison. Her breasts were mounds of desire. Her ears were beauteous earrings by themselves. Her face itself was a lesson of passion and her nose was as straight as a forefinger. Her cheeks were as tender as flowers and forehead resembled a garden in full bloom. Dark eyes were darker than the night, lips like two flower buds kept in a porcelain dish and tresses resembled nooses for admirers. Her arms were like tortured lightening. One would need a treasure of terms to describe her beauty from head to toe. Her exquisiteness far surpassed the beauty of others, who made the world beautiful. She was famously known as Umrao Umda Khanum Wali. Her comeliness was beyond anyone else's in this world. The moment we saw each other, we were both struck by the (Cupid's) arrow of love. That moment, accompanied by the sound of *sarod*[81] playing, created a strange and wondrous atmosphere. Such a pleasurable and delightful moment had never been attained before.

The very next day, that beloved of mine, in a most romantic and seductive manner, wondrously said to me, "I am in a most wretched condition due to my love for you, which I find irresistible. I suggest that something be done so that this moment will become memorable. I will be your servant for life; my heart is not permitting me to stay away from you any longer."

On hearing this delightful and emphatic proposal from her and I covered my eyes with my own hands which meant that I accepted her proposal. As I feared my father, I discussed this issue with my close confidantes. Eventually, it was proposed to obtain the assistance of *maulanas*, who possessed knowledge of the *Sharia.*[64]

The proposal being acceptable, I searched out and discussed with Mir Mohammad Mehdi, the *daroga*[33] of the court about Sayyed Ibrahim Ali (Bahadur). Applications were submitted for both *talāq*[83] on one side and *mut'ah*[84] marriage on the other. In this entire episode, the *daroga*, Mir Mehdi made great efforts, as a result of which, my plans could succeed. In this manner, the way to obtain the hand of this belle was cleared, and I gave her the title of Sikandar Begum.

As a matter of fact, she was a very bashful woman. After coming to me, she never ever conducted herself in a way over which someone could object. After some time, taking the excuse of presenting a *mujra*[85], her mother, Umda Khanum, presented herself before the royal court and, finding an opportunity, complained to my father that his son, the heir apparent, had confined her daughter in his household. My father, who was famous for his sense of fair-play, accordingly ordered that Umrao should present herself at the court. I rushed to my mother and pleaded that the girl was my *mut'ah* wife and I loved her from the bottom of my heart, and that I had not committed any atrocities on her. Meanwhile, this paragon of grace and devotion presented herself in court, weeping all the while. For her, this imminent separation from me was intolerable, but there was no other option.

As for me, I shed impotent tears, sometimes laughing aloud like a madman. Occasionally, I would loiter on the streets and at other times, I would shut myself in my room and keep to myself. When that perennial flower presented herself before my father, her mother was also nearby. After prolonged deliberations, the lady in question stated that if she was permitted to carry out unethical activities, she would go with her mother; however, if she was ordered to lead a virtuous life, then she would prefer to accompany Ibrahim (her former husband). Furthermore, the mother, Umda would have no claim on her in future, and if she made any claim or complaint, she (the mother) would be liable to be fined and punished as well.

Death of Imaman

With wine infused with the liqueur obtained from the flowers of love, all of a sudden, I was made aware of the inauspicious news regarding the death of Imaman, my friend and confidant. I immersed myself in the river of pain and a new grief suffused my heart. Her demise was a thorn which pierced my bosom. Gatherings which had been filled with ecstasy due to the charisma of such individuals fell silent.

Mohammad Kaharin

In the initial days of myself being the successor designate (to the throne), a maidservant had been appointed, to take care of my day-to-day requirements. Of pleasant disposition, she possessed a dusky complexion and was from the *kahar*[86] community. Earlier, she had been employed in the court of (late) Nasir-ud-Din Haider[2]. I felt like making her the target of my lust. She agreed but on the condition that she would be inducted as a regular maid in my household.

I agreed to her proposal and honoured her with the title of Behatar un-Nisan Khanum. My heart brimmed with passion for her, but she refused to be part of my harem. On enquiring from her about the reason for her choice, she burst into tears. One day, my anger at her intransigence made me order to have her dismissed, but she created such a hue-and-cry that I immediately reversed my decision.

She was a strange woman; although a maidservant after all, her love for me bordered on insanity, and yet, she had sworn not to become part of my harem. I kept plying her with gifts and costly dresses. This was because I was also infatuated with her. The same woman was responsible for serving me my meals twice a day.

Shah Baksh

In those days, a seventeen years old girl joined my harem, courtesy *Khas Mahal*[10]. She was inducted among those who had the privilege of serving the king in his private moments. She was a spry and cunning woman. I never liked her and did not even permit her to sit opposite me. Her job was to simply carry out the work assigned to her post. She was given the title of Shah Baksh.

Altaf Baksh

Through the good offices of *Khas Mahal,* another seventeen year old came into my contact. She was also inducted in the category of attendants and given the title of Altaf Baksh.

Undoubtedly, she was a very beautiful woman, but did not hold any attraction for me. She was not allowed to sit in my presence. She remained confined to the household work assigned to her, and failed to take up lessons in music or educate herself.

Shirin Habshin

Through the good offices of Mohammad Hussain Ali Khan, a *Habshin*[87] called Shirin entered my household. She too was inducted among the other attendants of the household.

Fiza Habshin

Another *Habshin* joined my household, through Shirin (above). She was given the name of Fiza and inducted among other attendants.

Laila Habshin

Laila, another *Habshin* joined my services through Shirin.

A Gift from Hazrat Jannat Makān[149]

In those very days, one of the *begums* of (late) Nasir-ud-Din Haider expired, and from her estate, six female attendants were also confiscated. These were benignly reassigned to me by my father. Two, I retained as my personal attendants, and the remaining four were married off by me. Those who joined my service were renamed as Farkhanda Baksh and Shah Baksh. This was the same Shah Baksh, whose daughter, Shams Ara Begum died during childbirth. And for this reason, she was awarded the title of Farkhanda Khanum Saheba and kept in seclusion. But what can be done for someone whose fortunes are not favourable, and her daughter, Shams Ara did not survive. Otherwise the title of *Mahal* would have been bestowed upon her.

Aloofness of Nawab Khas Mahal

With the grace of the Almighty, whose glory extends from the heavens above to the earth below, this *Parikhana* saw significant progress. Its cultural gatherings evoked a strange desire in the heart, an electric warmth in one's ears. The *paris* of my *Parikhana* had become so adept in their craft that the celestial nymphs from Lord Indra's court[88] and famed fairies of the Caucasian mountains, would have faced a serious challenge. Each and every *pari* had the seductiveness to shatter the hearts of human spectators. And I could entirely perceive the proficiency therein. If I could free myself from one attractive seductress, I would get entangled in the mortal coils of another. Without them, even day-to-day activities would be colourless and devoid of pleasure. Some of these *paris* were elevated to the status of *mahals*. The huntress was successful in ensnaring her prey. Actually, each and every *pari* had me captured with her charms. I was never assailed by feelings of melancholy or dejection at any point of time. But yes, one or two unfortunate incidents did occur. These include the unfortunate demise of *daroga* Najm un-Nisa, secondly, the death of my close confidante, Imaman and thirdly, the passing away of an infant daughter. Otherwise, I was totally unaware of grief and dejection.

This preoccupation of mine in matters of love and passion was intolerable to the other *begums*. Especially Nawab Khas Mahal, in whose heart burnt a fire of misery and malice. She would taunt one *pari* and reproach another; criticize someone's attire and disparage someone else's adornments. She would behave strangely, so much so that sometimes she would start an altercation spontaneously; her behaviour irked every other woman in the vicinity. Like her, others also held the title of *begums*, but I could not devote much time to them. They were also very envious and they remained obsessed with the ornamentation and adornment of the *paris*.

Weary of it all, I assigned the duty of the *paris'* day-to-day dressing and adornment to *daroga* Mohammad Hussain Ali Khan and simultaneously gave him the title of Mohammad Moat-mud Ali Khan. He very happily accepted the title and strove hard to fulfil his responsibilities. I also appreciated his hard work and felt that he fully deserved the privileges given to him. From the start to the end, he never made any mistake on his duties. Although he did commit one blunder, the details of which I shall mention in an appropriate time.

Khwajasārā Rehan

Mohammad Moat-mud Ali Khan, an eunuch recommended a person called Rehan to me. I accepted his proposal and appointed the latter as an attendant. He had earlier served the *khwajasaras* in the service of Saifulla Hamir Hadi's *begums*. He was of Abyssinian origin, slimly built, with gentle manners and a silent disposition. He was totally devoid of any ego problems and was about forty years of age. I gave him the title of Mohammad Rehan Ali Khan. Because of his diligent work, he became worthy of the ruler's favours.

Contingent of Female Horse Riders

A person by the name of Haji[89] Sharif entered my services on the recommendation of Mohammad Moat-mud Ali Khan. He had earlier served the *khwajasaras* in the service of Saifulla Hamir Hadi. He was also around forty years old. He was a peace-loving and gentle soul. He never did anything which was irksome to me. He would promptly carry out my orders. He was given the responsibility of being the *daroga* of the *zenana* after being honored by the title of Mohammad Sharif Ali Khan. He performed his duties in an appropriate manner.

During this time, I felt that guards should be appointed for my residence. But I was helpless due to lack of finances and uncontrolled spending. Also, my father had not permitted the same. Out of sheer desperation, thirty female guards were appointed for the security of the *zenana*. Arrangements were also made for the daily parade of these women guards and acquaint them with *Farsi* language. So much so that in a short while, these women became so adept that in my opinion, the British parades became insignificant. Each and every woman was at par with the British soldiers in maintaining their arms and uniforms. Other than this, I appointed fifty horsemen, who were trained in parading and *Farsi*. This contingent was also far superior than their British counterparts.

Haji Mohammad Sharif Ali Khan was appointed as officer for both these contingents. The title of Janbaz Sarkar Mirza Wali Ahad Bahadur Karnail Haji Mohammad Sharif Ali Khan was simultaneously bestowed upon him. Actually, he trained (the contingents) in parade with great effort and hard work. The parade horses appeared like a wall of iron. This person never accepted a single paisa as a bribe. His awe-inspiring presence was such that no soldier dared to talk to another in the parade grounds.

Visit to Shrines on Pilgrimage

Other than the eunuchs Bashir Ali Khan and Feroz Ali Khan, my honourable father had provided another eunuch by the name of Bilal, as my attendant, who was without any specific duty. One day he expressed his desire to be relieved so he could proceed on a pilgrimage to holy shrines. I granted his request and also gave him rupees two thousand towards expenses.

Subsequently, I was informed that Yasmin Pari, Mahrukh Pari and Sardar Pari had also tearfully expressed the desire to proceed on pilgrimage. Since I had acquired them after great effort, I was not willing to let them proceed on such a long journey, and I also could not believe that these women had expressed such a desire. However, I was convinced after having enquired from them, face-to-face. But I was irked at this unfaithfulness and discussed it with all and sundry. Eventually, I was exasperated and made arrangements for them to live separately and henceforth, never ever allowed them in my presence. But I was greatly anguished by all this. Meanwhile, *khwajasārā* Bilal returned from pilgrimage. However, after six months, he again expressed the desire to visit *Karbala*. I gladly accepted his proposal and again gave him a sum of rupees two thousand towards expenses. At the same time, I also permitted these three *paris* to proceed on pilgrimage, and granted an amount of rupees four thousand towards expenses for the journey. This was because it was foolish to retain them any longer in my service. But God knows, what crossed their hearts and they hesitated to finally proceed. It appears that because they had lost their position due to their wish (to proceed on pilgrimage), they now vacillated in visiting the same place.

Eventually Bilal proceeded alone on his pilgrimage. After that incident, I developed an aversion for these three *paris* and no longer respected or desired them as before. There did not seem to be any reason to maintain intimacy with them. Later, they tried various ruses to lure me, but I remained alert every time and did not accept them at any cost. They would arrive to train others in the training center, and did not have any loss of status, compared to others. Only I did not give them any attention. The moment I glanced at their faces, I was reminded of their perfidy.

This was the same Yasmin Pari, for whom, besotted with love, I had tearfully narrated my helplessness. It was God's strange will that now her condition would be reduced to this.

Courtiers and Religious Beliefs (*Shi'ism*)

Gradually my acquaintance with courtiers who belonged to the *Sunni* sect, including Ghulam Raza, increased. In addition to this, my *ustād*[90], Qutub Ali Khan was also from the same sect. Day and night I pondered that if they too adopted my faith (*Shi'ism*), it would have pleased me greatly. However, on probing their bent of mind, I realised that they were too deeply ingrained with their beliefs and would never convert.

It was the monsoon season. One day, with great politeness and in a gentle manner, I asked them to convert. Maybe it was God's will that my plan could reach its logical conclusion. All accepted my request. Immediately, I arranged a carriage for them, to seek the blessings of *Mujtahid*[91] Sultan-ul-Ulema Maulvi Sayyid Mohammad. After reaching there, all of them became devout

Shi'as, and returned with a message from the *Ulema,* indicating their conversion to a superior faith. On seeing this, I was overjoyed and conferred them with titles and gifts. The titles were as follows:

- Title of Ghulam Yadullah Khan to Qutub Ali Khan
- Title of Ghulam Ali Khan to Nathu Khan *alias* Ghulam Raza Khan
- Title of Ghulam Hasan Khan to Gehman Khan, a relative of Ghulam Raza Khan

They also took an oath that henceforth, they were the true servants of *Huzur-e-wala*[92] and would follow His footsteps during their lifetime. On hearing these words, I touched my breast in reverence, indicating that I had accepted their supplication. Accordingly, I took utmost care of them. As far as I can remember, I never shirked my responsibility towards them.

Appraisal (Assessment) of *Musahibs*[93]

One day I was in *Hazrat Bagh*. Everywhere, there were droplets of rain from merciful clouds. Colourful flowers blossomed all around. The fragrance from the flowers of *Raat ki Rani*[94] assailed the senses. It was close to midnight. I was seated in *Bangla Falak Sair.* In my attendance were present, my close friends and confidants, Ghulam Raza Khan, Chajju Khan, Sabit Ali Khan, Ghulam Yadullah Khan and others. All of them kept me entertained with interesting anecdotes and hilarious jokes. At this moment, I felt that this was the appropriate time to assess their devotion for me. I called forth one near me and whispered in his ear that he should send an impersonator in my presence - someone who appeared wounded and brandish an unsheathed sword. I wanted to see the devotion of these converted friends. On hearing my order, that person went away. After some time, an impersonator, bleeding profusely and holding a naked sword entered the terrace by way of the staircase. Immediately, on entering, he tried to attack me. I expressed fake agony and surprise. On seeing my distress, Ghulam Raza Khan caught him by the waist and wanted to dispatch him with his own sword. When I saw this conduct of his, I was alarmed and exclaimed, "Stop! Stop! He is an impersonator. Please don't kill him." By this time, the impersonator was also loudly protesting that he was innocent. On hearing all this, he was immediately released. Afterwards, it was observed that during the scuffle, the impersonator had been wounded in many places on his body. Immediately, I gave an appropriate reward to him and appointed him as an attendant; I also awarded rupees five hundred to each braveheart. Other than this, each one was gifted a pistol and a gun and honoured with appropriate titles like *Musahebani Khas* and *Jawanen Pehra*. After that incident, whenever I went to repose in my private apartments, these special companions would be on guard. They were also on my security detail, when I would be asleep in the palace.

Birth of Mirza Birjis Qadr

Another incident from my happy days. One day, I got the news that a new flower was about to bloom in my garden. The news that Mehak Pari was expecting was truly gladdening. On hearing the good news, I thanked God and had Mehak Pari (Begum Hazrat Mahal) confined, after honouring her with the title of *Iftikhar un-Nisa*. After the term of her pregnancy was over, she gave birth to a worthy son. His grandfather was overjoyed; eleven cannons were fired on the occasion and the child was named Mirza Birjis Qadr Bahadur by him. On my part, a celebration was organised; singers and dancers entranced intoxicatingly. In this event, each and every *pari* had decked herself up like a bride. When the *paris* danced, the audience cheered with their each and every seductive move.

Jahanara Begum

Another auspicious news spread good cheer in my life. This time, Fiza Habshin announced her pregnancy. Immediately I expressed my gratitude at the *dargah* and sent Fiza for confinement. A pearl of desires was born, whom my father named as Jahanara Begum Saheba, may Allah grant her a long life.

An Incident of Yasmin Pari and Sarfaraz Pari

One day, it was rumoured that both Yasmin Pari and Sarfaraz Pari were expecting, and as per custom, I had them confined. But after a few days, it was revealed to be just a conjecture. They were brought out of confinement and kept busy in dancing lessons and sarod playing.

Feminine Recalcitrance of Hur Pari

Subsequently, I got the news that Hur Pari was expecting. Although I was overjoyed at the news, having being been deceived earlier by the incident of Yasmin Pari and Sarfaraz Pari, I was not very convinced. She was sent for confinement after a period of five months. But that woman could not endure confinement and kept on weeping, although I tried to convince her to the best of my ability. I reasoned that perhaps she was unable to bear the separation from me. But it was mere speculation on my part. Even after being consoled and comforted in every manner, she would bluntly state that she would not tolerate confinement at any cost. And if she was forced to remain so, she would abort the child.

On hearing this, I tried to reason with her that it was a great sin to take a life like this. Eventually, she gave birth to a premature male child after seven months of pregnancy. The infant survived for a mere forty days. I permitted her to take up singing and dancing lessons once again, wearing the garments of mourning. But she would outwardly weep in front of others and express her desire to leave. *Lā hawla wa lā quwwat*[57]!!

Pregnancy of Haidri

Daroga Najm un-Nisa Begum had left behind two female attendants. One was named Mamman, and the other was called Haidri. Mamman was married off by Ghulam Haider, whereas Haidri was retained in his own retinue of servants. After some time, Haidri was reported to be pregnant. I was bewildered and annoyed at this, and whip in hand, I proceeded to ascertain the truth. She would name various people (responsible for her situation). When I threatened her with the whip, she confessed that she was pregnant with Sabit Ali Khan's child. This was completely unacceptable to me. Immediately, I enquired from the four brothers. They fell at my feet and said that if any evidence was found of this, they were ready to present themselves to me for beheading. That God only knew whose child it was. That they had been falsely implicated. After all this breast-beating and commotion, it was decided that only after the dismissal of Haidri would this matter subside. One of her brothers was employed as a *farrash*[95] in my establishment, having been adopted earlier by *daroga* Najm un-Nisa Begum. I handed over the custody of Haidri to him and pardoned the four brothers.

Bilquis Pari

I had become quite enamoured with Bilquis Pari because of her good looks and glances which seemed to pierce my heart. Her coquettishness captivated me. Her slightest degree of coyness made me distraught. When she sang, I would weep, and when she danced, I would sit with my head bowed. When she busied herself with her training, I would be lost in her liveliness. I would remain awake while she slept and when she was awake, instead of appreciating my feelings, she would unjustifiably taunt me by saying, "You desire so-and-so; you love so-and-so more than me." I would massage her legs all night. My days would pass in gazing at her. While eating, she would offer to share with me the most ordinary of items, which I would accept with alacrity without hesitation. I would follow here wherever she went and stand near her, when she sat down. In a nutshell, she had made me her besotted lover. She would change her dresses several times in a day. The essence of *henna* suffused her body, her teeth shone brightly, lips were stained red with *paan* and her forehead shone with the application of glitter powder. Her hair would sometimes be coiled and sometimes be straight; hands would be hennaed and fingers embellished with rings.

One day, after much discussion amongst themselves, (late) *daroga* Najm un-Nisa Begum, Umda Mahal and Nishat Mahal, invited me to a room in *Shahanshah Manzil*. On reaching there, I understood that they wanted to convey something to me. I queried, "What do you want to say?" At this, all three started discussing my fondness for Sarfaraz Pari, including the narration of some unfortunate *jumlas*[96] also. They would pound their thighs and clench their teeth in grief. Becoming impatient at all this, I exclaimed, "For the sake of God, please say what you wanted to tell, so my patience is not tested further." I wanted to know the reason for their grief, but they continued to behave erratically. Eventually, I swore an oath, after which *daroga* Najm un-Nisa Begum started her lament like this: "O *Jān-é-Alam*[97]! You are enamoured by Sarfaraz Pari to such an extent, but there are strange rumours floating about her." On hearing this, I replied, "Please complete your statement. Why do you trouble me by this incomplete information."

In one voice, *daroga* Najm un-Nisa Begum, and the other *paris* asserted, " O *Jān-é-Alam*, we are devoted to you. The female sex invariably has some drawbacks. If you are not angered, I would like to tell you that outwardly, although it appears that Sarfaraz Pari loves you very much, the facts are very much to the contrary and she does not care for you at all."

On hearing these words about Sarfaraz Pari, my face darkened with anguish, my heart beat erratically and my eyes filled with tears. I replied, "You all are witness that I never lacked in my devotion for Sarfaraz. In this situation, why did she choose the path of perfidy?" All of a sudden, the thought crossed my mind that since all my *begums* were jealous of Sarfaraz, it would not be surprising if these accusations were false. Thereupon, I asked them, "All right, tell me, what is the solution to all this?" They replied that I should bide my time, and with God's grace, they would provide proof of her unfaithfulness to me. One day, I gathered all the *paris* at one place and addressed them:

"O my companions! I did not keep any of you in my household, against your wish. Some of you came because of your love for me. Others saw me in their dreams, and submitted themselves to me. Somebody saw me passing by in the *bazaar* and suffered the pangs of love in their heart, while others expressed their love for me, right here in my home. Someone forgot herself in the rhythm of dance while another lost consciousness in music and song. But lately, I have been hearing disturbing news. God forbid such a situation should arise in which I would be reduced to a personification of dejection and disappointment." After saying this, I started weeping uncontrollably and turning towards Sarfaraz Pari, I spoke the following words:

"The Lord knows that the respite from this condition of mine is in your hands. I have not kept you in imprisonment. You can say whatever you want. I am ready to submit to all your demands, fulfil all your desires unquestioningly. I am responsible for all of you *begums* and *paris*. But for God's sake, do not commit any indiscretion, which would tarnish your image and label you as ungrateful." On hearing this, all the women present, swearing on their allegiance and trustworthiness, stated in one voice, "May we be struck with blindness, if we have served any one else other than your good-self." Sarfaraz Pari and Hur Pari were especially emphatic on their loyalty. My tears were unstoppable. Eventually the fire raging in my breast subsided, but I continued to remain apprehensive.

Convergence of My Companions

I continued to be very much perturbed over the events narrated above. My heart remained engulfed in sorrow all the time. One day, in anger, I took all the companions and *begums* of *Shahanshah Manzil* to task and narrated my woes to them; that I could no longer be patient over the narrative of *daroga* Najm un-Nisa Begum and other two. Several took oaths of loyalty after hearing my anguish. They said, "It is not proper to suspect us based on heresy. We will never hesitate even to be beheaded to prove our loyalty." I replied, "Loyalty and respect are gifts from the Almighty. God forbid, any sign of disloyalty should reflect upon your brows. If it happens, it would be a sign of disloyalty to the very salt you owe your existence to." When everybody started inquiring as to who was responsible for spreading such canards, I candidly mentioned the name of the above *paris* and *daroga* Najm un-Nisa. After that day, a lot of rivalry arose between them. Till the day of death, this mutual discord continued.

After their denials, I pardoned everyone, but deep inside my heart, the anxiety remained. Unfortunately, I kept my patience for some more days, otherwise I would have seen everything unfold before my very eyes.

Mir Ahmed Ali and Mir Gauhar Ali

In those days, Mir Ahmed Ali, a reader of *marsiyas*[98] and his son, Mir Gauhar Ali joined my services. They were adept in singing the *dhrupad raag*[99]. Gauhar Ali, by virtue of being my pupil in music, became highly respected in my service. Gradually, his interaction with me increased. The situation became such that he would join me unhesitatingly, whether I was by myself or with company. He did not face any hindrance in openly expressing his views and I would also accept them forthwith. One day he presented a memorandum to me. It stated:

"O Protector of the World! After kissing the ground (in respect), I would like to state that this servant of your is unable to bear the predicament of the *paris* any longer. I pray that your Highness shall not delay enquiring into the matter. After that, the seriousness of the situation shall be obvious to you."

On reading this petition, I was angered that although the *paris* had denied everything and had asked for forgiveness, they were still engaged in the same objectionable activities. The old scars of my heart were left bleeding afresh. I again enquired diligently in a gathering of the *paris* and other attendants, but they all denied any indiscretion, banging their heads in shame. Both Sarfaraz Pari and Hur Pari exclaimed, "If there is anyone present who has actually witnessed any disloyalty, then that person may please catch us red-handed; then only we shall confess our crime. Unless you, honoured sir, see any indiscretion with your own eyes, please do not believe the words of others. If any person claims that he can prove us guilty, let him present his evidence before your honourable person."

I felt silent on hearing this argument. Subsequently, I dismissed Gauhar Ali from service, because it was possible that he had been hatching some conspiracy in this matter. But even then, my mind remained agitated with doubts and suspicion. As a result of all this, my health deteriorated and I started suffering from palpitations of the heart. Considering that I was still a youth, immersing myself in song and dance performances of the *paris* would refresh my mind and give me relief. But I would remain sorrowful. Because there was no one with whom I could confide to. Those whom I had thought to be my friends, did not prove to be genuine. This was the reality of my confidants and bosom women friends. My parents never enquired about my welfare. And there were wives, who repelled me. Not only this - in those days, I became so weakened that even my day-to-day movements had become restricted. I would offer *namaz*[100] while seated. Thrice, I fell ill in this manner and was bedridden for six months. Allah have mercy on me!

She Was My Exclusive Beloved

When the deceit of Sarfaraz Pari had reached its zenith, my obsession for her also started waning, and it was so traumatic for me that I started behaving erratically. Sometimes I would roam in the forest and on other occasions, would take a ride down the river. Returning home in great sadness and unrest, I would be beset by bizarre apprehensions. In my solitude, I would agonizingly remember her deceit and would sometimes just peer at my own visage in the mirror for hours.

One day, Rashq Pari sensing my anguish, expressed her sympathies. She really served me well, may the Lord bless her. She exclaimed, " O *Jān-é-Alam*! *Sadke jawaan*[101], why are you beset with such grief and restlessness?

I replied, "O my faithful beloved, you are well aware of Sarfaraz Pari's conduct. If you have any information in that regard, please enlighten me, so this agony in my heart may be pacified." At this she laughed aloud and replied," O my innocent Master, of that treacherous woman, I know very well, but you should not torture yourself so much because of her. One should keep one's soul spotless like a freshly bloomed rose. God willing, I will expose her shenanigans to you one day." I responded, "O my love, my faithful one, whatever you know, please tell me this very instant." At this, she recounted the same duplicity of Sarfaraz Pari, which I had heard earlier. This narration pained me even more; in the name of Allah, just what was the issue? Here I was, ready to sacrifice myself for her charms, and yet, there was so much duplicity hidden away. I probed Rashq Pari thoroughly in this matter, and she related such incidents that I was left speechless. From that moment, I developed a hatred for all the *paris*, other than Rashq Pari, for whom I developed a deep feeling of affection. Because now she was my confidant and lover. And due to this, I would discuss this problem only with her.

There is no doubt that sometimes she would denounce Sarfaraz and others, out of sheer resentment and envy. Even then, I was already in the throes of her love, and would hang on to her each and every word. I would embrace her sometimes, telling her that she was my special love, and if she also responded, I was ready to become her slave. Accordingly, she assured me that she would gather all the facts and started to keep track of everyone.

Sarfaraz Pari's Disclosure

One night, Dildar Pari was giving me company. On finding

solitude, she engaged on the topic of Sarfaraz Pari's indiscretions and said:

"O *Jān-é-Alam*! You are so very guileless! The women are engaged in something or the other and you are immersed in your passion for them. For God's sake, please open your eyes now and observe what is happening around you. You are oblivious in your own house, and squandering lakhs of rupees. If you had maintained a relationship with me, instead of the others, the situation would not have taken this turn. You have still not understood your untrustworthy lovers." It was true that Dildar Pari was a pious woman, with the habits of angels and pure inside. She was cheerful, exquisitely beautiful, with a body like a *houri*[102] , and feet as delicate as flowers; on whose every coquettish action, I was willing to sacrifice myself a hundred times. When I noticed that such a *pari* desired me, I accepted her forthwith. But even then, the hypocrisy of the times were heavy upon me.

My grief over Sarfaraz Pari had transformed my breast into a limestone kiln. My devotion for her was decreasing, and yet, an uneasiness clouded my eyes twenty fours hours a day. One day, I clutched at her hand and said accusingly, "O soul of my life.. you have caused me unnecessary agony. Is this fair that you made someone desperate for your love and then you became aloof yourself. I deeply regret this sad adultery on your part. All is not lost, for the sake of God Almighty, please retrace your steps."

However, she again swore on her loyalty and trust-worthiness, declaring her boundless love for me. During this conversation, she would sometimes laugh and sometimes weep, and accuse me, "You do not love me. It's good that you were punished." She would reach out sometimes and give a serving of *pān* to another *pari*, all the while averting her eyes from me.

One day I took a finger ring from her, with a vow that I would heat it red hot and brand myself with it. When I got up for morning *namaz*, I thought of heating the ring in the embers of the *hookah*[103], before branding myself with it. But because the ring belonged to a deceitful woman, I could not bring myself to do it.

Holding the ring in one hand, I heated the mouthpiece of the *hookah* and branded my left thigh at eight places with it. Still, the flames of passion in my heart could not be extinguished. After some days, I approached that double-crossing lover by profession and stated, "O you beauty who inflicts torture, see what I have done in my passion for you." On seeing the blisters on my thigh, she chortled, laughing out aloud, and kissed my wounds. And yet, there was no change in her attitude or deplorable behaviour.

Love On The Path of Oppression

After some time had passed, that unfaithful, sadistic and double-crossing woman, who was extremely proud of her physical charms said, " O *Jān-é-Alam,* o oblivious person, do you know that in your love, I too have faced burn injuries on my thigh?" I wept when I saw the burn marks on her thighs, which resembled blooming flowers.

I was astonished that on one hand, her betrayal knew no bounds, and on the other hand, she displayed her love in such a manner. After all, what was the meaning of this duplicity? To cut a long story short, I kissed her wounds, brushing them with my eyelashes, and telling her that she had copied me entirely. She replied in verse, implying that the copy was better than the original. On realising this, I fell silent. Afterwards, I was informed by Dildar Pari and Rashq Pari that these wounds had been inflicted for the sole reason of convincing me that she was true to me. On hearing this, I was again plunged in the maelstrom of uncertainty and doubts and started to bite my hands with my teeth. After great effort, I went to her and said, "O unkind and unfaithful.. you declare your love with fake actions. O deceitful, you are still not in control of your hypocrisy and treachery." At this, she replied, "Nobody wounds his or her own body without good reason. This is an expression of pure passion." This argument of hers was very convincing, as it encompassed her love and emotions. My heart grew heavy and I started banging my head on the doorway. If she had not caught hold of me, my skull would have been fractured for sure.

All said and done, I remained in this strange dilemma day and night, contemplating on her actions, her deceit, her love and her passion; hoping against hope that I would be able to eventually see through her veiled personality and learn about her reclusive existence.

Dildar Pari Expresses Love

Dildar Pari was madly in love with me and I too had opened the doors of my heart to her. As a result of this, even food and drink became anathema to me in her absence. I would frequently sleep with my head resting on her lap, but after I became close to Sarfaraz Pari, my infatuation for Dildar reduced somewhat. However, she remained a forceful contender for my affections. One day she sobbed, "You are totally oblivious of me." I replied, "I am oblivious of myself, so how am I supposed to be aware of others?" She retorted, "O heartless person, I branded myself on the thigh with a hot ring, as an expression of my adulation for you, but you remain totally unaware of this. At least provide me some soothing emollient, which I can apply on my burns."

I perceived that indeed there were burn marks on her thigh. I felt sad and exclaimed, "After all, what happened to you so that you had to take this drastic step? She replied, "Whatever has happened is for the good. Please do not worry." Despite all this, neither I felt any ardour for her, nor did she take any extra care of me.

A Fight between Mashuq-e-Khas and Sarfaraz Pari

When Sarfaraz Pari came to know about these developments through her informers, she became livid with rage. On every occasion and in every gathering, she would outpour her feelings and anguish. She also had a severe altercation with Mashuq-e-

Khas when the latter developed an inclination towards me. The situation deteriorated to such an extent that the two actually had a brawl, pulling each others' hair braids in the process. This free-for-all scrap started in the morning and continued till noon. When I observed that Mashuq-e-Khas was getting injured by the kicks delivered by Sarfaraz, I rushed to the scene of the cat fight and pacified the two, bringing the confrontation to an end.

But Mashuq-e-Khas held on to my collar and blurted out, "Now things have come to such a pass that you have me humiliated through your favourite women. I will not stay here a minute longer." I tried to reason with her that this was a mere figment of her imagination, but she would not budge. Because she was determined to leave, I ordered a carriage for her. I could not fathom her anger, but I was helpless before her fury. Ultimately, she boarded the carriage and hurriedly departed.

I was overcome with sorrow and sobbed loudly. I was in a strange dilemma: on one side, the fear of my parents prevailed, and on the other, my uncontrollable adulation for Mashuq-e-Khas continued. As I mulled over my unenviable situation, an attendant entered and informed me that Mashuq-e-Khas had only proceeded till the poultry coop; she had then returned to her living quarters. Overjoyed, I expressed my gratitude to the Almighty[104].

Sarfaraz Pari Leaves in a Huff

The return of Mashuq-e-Khas made Sarfaraz Pari furious, and now she expressed her desire to leave. She also approached a well, with the intention of committing suicide by drowning herself in it, but was prevented from doing so by some bystanders. I went up to her and tried to reason with her, but she was adamant to return to her home. It was a strangely difficult situation. Finally, out of exasperation, I burst out, "Why do you issue threats? If you want to go, then please go." Hearing this, she boarded the carriage and went off. After her departure, I hung a portrait of her around my neck and sat down in the doorway of the building. I was convinced that Sarfaraz, being deceitful by nature, would not make a re-entry here. I felt like weeping uncontrollably. I would alternately stare at my own burn wounds and then kiss her portrait. In desperation, I sat like this for a full four hours. All of a sudden, I saw her approaching me. I ran to her and embraced her passionately. She held onto me, sobbing incessantly. We sat like this for a long time in solitude. After asking for forgiveness, I started talking to her in an amorous manner. When Mashuq-e-Khas came to know of these developments, the flame of covetousness started blazing in her heart.

Sultan Pari

Out of sheer grudge, the accusation of infidelity had also been heaped upon Sultan Pari. But I was convinced that she was truly faithful to me. When she came to know of these false accusations against her, she wept day and night in great agitation, which affected her health adversely. In dejection, she also stopped eating and drinking, and grew feeble day by day. Unable to control her anger and dejection, she took my official seal (of Crown Prince), and after heating it red hot, marked her thigh in three places with it. Then limping badly, she approached me. On my enquiring about her gait, she handed me the seal saying, "I am ready to sacrifice myself for you. You have included me among deceitful and faithless people, but see the condition of my thigh?" I was flabbergasted on seeing the glowing impressions of my seal on the flesh of her thigh. I expressed my regret, after which she embraced me and sobbed uncontrollably. After this incident, my feelings towards her became crystal clear.

Umrao Baksh

A woman called Umrao Baksh joined my establishment through the good offices of Amman. She seemed to have a preliminary knowledge of music. After two months, she became pregnant and had to be put in confinement by me.

Adornment of *Huzur Bagh*

From the very beginning, I appreciated cleanliness, but other than this, I excelled in making new discoveries and constructing new buildings. Consequently, I felt the need to embellish a garden and lay its water channels. Initially, I thought of creating two streams. One would be named *Chashm-e-Shireen* and the other would be called *Chashm-e-Faiz*[105]. A keeper was also appointed by me for this. The person proved to be extremely resourceful and capable. In a short while, after arranging everything, he had the garden inspected by me. I christened the garden as *Huzur Bagh*. It was a fact that such a garden with such streams of water was not to be seen, other than in this kingdom. Be it any season, the garden would be extremely relaxing. It had a small building in its centre, equipped with a little water tank, which was decorated with flower pots. In the summers, there would be no better place than this, to spend one's hours. God only knows how it was so breezy, but when the sun would be at its peak, and people would be distressed like fishes out of water, this place would remain suffused with a strange coolness. The floor of this building was made of marble.

A person by the name of Ali Beg was appointed as *daroga* of the premises, through the good offices of Ali Naqi Khan. The garden's *Chashm-e-Shireen* stream was of forty *gaj*[106] and the second stream, *Chashm-e-Faiz* was around ten to fifteen *gaj* in size, with fountains on both sides. The joy of the monsoons would be experienced when these fountains operated. Marble benches had been provided everywhere. Flower gardens bloomed with different varieties of flowers. It was an impossibility that a garden containing rose shrubs would have climber roses and vice versa. Everywhere, one could see porcelain urns and vases made of stone, which had plants inside them, and yet, not a drop of water fell down from these.

Below the trees, marble stools had been kept for one to relax on. Every corner of the garden was decked up with jasmine plants. Each flower garden was provided with protective barriers and tall trees, among which there was a mulberry tree, the size of which I had never seen elsewhere. Below this, a marble pavilion had been provided, so one could sit here and enjoy the joys of the rainy season. Every Friday, there was a gathering of *paris* and singing girls beneath this tree. Melodious birds and dazzling peacocks made this tree their home. No hunting was permitted in this garden. Khan Sahib, who had proved his efficiency, and also due to the fact that he was obliged to me, had become quite close to me. But, regrettably, he started to interfere in my personal affairs.

Observing all this, *daroga* Mir Mehdi became envious, and unnecessarily became his adversary. Ali Naqi Khan was somewhat bald-headed. One day, I jokingly said, "Nawab Sahib, being bald is a sign that one day you shall become *Wazir*." He replied that it may be entirely possible through my good grace. I was somewhat perturbed at this and mentally addressed the Lord thus, "Ya Allah, I did not want to make a false statement. With Your Will, one day my words shall ring true."

Jogi and *Jogan*[107]

This is a narration of those times when the multitude of *paris*, the congregation of singers and my own amorous ways were at their peak. It would be difficult to differentiate between night and day. Melodious singers, adept musicians accompanied by percussion artists who were maestros in their own right - all playing till late into the night. Those were heady times. There was no other sorrow, other than the anguish of unrequited love. The lovers also experienced the same melancholy. They were also not aware of anything, other than sumptuous meals, costly dresses and melodious music. With the grace of God, like the benevolence of *Kamdhenu*[108], any kind of sorrow was non-existent. I would be mostly preoccupied and absorbed with the charms of one beauty or the other. The envious heavens themselves shed tears from the stars, which would drop on the earth below. The *houris* would observe my social gatherings with envious eyes.

The sky was overcast with clouds. A gentle drizzle falling on the leaves of trees created a wondrous sight. The rain-soaked breeze spread the intoxicating fragrance of flowers in all directions of *Huzur Bagh.* Birds perched on climbing roses sang in melodious tones. Industrious and persevering gardeners were engaged in clearing and maintaining the paths in the garden. The shrubs of *karaunda*[109] were especially dense with flowers and leaves. Rose beds presented an extremely tasteful and pleasant sight. The branches and leaves on the trees were innumerable. The orange trees were densely packed with fruit. The *kamrak*[110] trees, having tightly knit fronds, provided an impenetrable shadow, as if a green tent had been erected in the garden.

The garden had been provided with thousands of varieties of plants and trees. There was an exclusive orchard for apples. Another orchard was for peaches and a third for *karaunda.* Orchards for guavas and sweet oranges (including European variety) had also been created. Amazingly, all the trees were of the same height as the *Palmyra* trees present in the surroundings. Trunks of trees had been coloured, with great precision. Wild roses bloomed in another garden; their white flowers between green leaves shimmered like the stars in the heavens. There were flowerbeds of jasmine and chrysanthemums also - the yellow and white colours shone through like the sun and moon respectively.

The premises were provided with pathways, which essentially divided the garden into three segments, lying side by side. This arrangement also contained tall grass, which bent forward, as if embracing each other like lovers, producing a shade and cooling effect; hence the pathway came to be known as *Thandi Sadak*[111]. Broad leaves of banana plants were so closely entwined together that it was impossible for sunlight to filter through the gaps. Habitually careless, I was lounging in this shady area, engrossed in thoughts of love and separation; my own composition - *Afsanaye Ishq* was being recited. In this condition, suddenly I felt like disrobing myself like Majnu. I tore away my clothes and in this frenzied condition, walked by, oblivious of others present.

I had all the appurtenances of a *Jogi*. The ashes of pearls shone on my forehead like the sunrise. Wearing strings of pearls on their necks, Mashuq-e-Khas and Sikandar Mahal had assumed the role of *Jogans*. I had clasped their hands under my arms. All three of us were sheathed in sheets of cloth made in Benaras, and our faces were smeared with the ashes of charred pearls. The fragrance from our dishevelled tresses spread across the entire garden. Ears adorned with earrings and danglers, and throats embellished with strings of pearls. In this intoxicating gathering were present, my companions, attendants and enthusiasts of music and dance.

This intoxicating atmosphere enraptured each and every person present, so much so that everyone started tearing off their clothes in gay abandon. The various musical instruments, string and percussion thrilled into melody. Ecstatic singers sang in such a manner that their voices must have reached to the sky above. Those who were watching this spectacle were amazed and dumb-founded. The euphony of this throng did not spare anyone. There was no eye that was not tearful, no heart that was not restless and impatient. Waists draped with *dupatta*[112], decorated with lace were sharper than the sharpest eyes. May the evil eye spare the unique charms of ample bosoms and well proportioned arms. Statuesque legs resembled graceful tree trunks. Holding both *jogans* clasped on either side, the *jogi* passed swiftly by the people present in the gathering. Whoever came face to face also lost his senses. Men and women were in a swoon. Each and every eye was turned on the *jogi* and *jogans*. A multitude of women were present. The garden appeared to be an abode of fairies.

On entering through the gates of the garden, when Anees-ud-Daula and Razi-ud-Daula Bahadur witnessed this strange sight - amazed and stunned, they tore off their clothes. Smearing their face with ashes, they donned loin cloths and appeared in the garb of *jogis*. Whomsoever witnessed this astonishing spectacle was convinced that a scene from the heavens was being re-enacted on earth. As dusk approached, everyone in a body proceeded towards one corner of the garden. Singers with magic in their voices presented a *khayal.*[113]

"Do not romance with your lover, I am a jogan (ascetic) *now"*

The *Jogi* was sitting cross-legged, with a supple body and chest exposed through torn garments - whoever perceived this vision remained utterly bewildered and astounded. Both *jogans* presented an incredible sight. They were engrossed in a dance form that resembled the intertwined boughs of grape trees; their mind-blowing rendition of love songs and dancing all reduced the audience to tears.

As the sun descended below the horizon and twilight set in, the *jogi* all at once arose from his seat, and gathering his musical instruments, walked away, finally settling down in *Rafat Manzil* above the stream. Lights resembling the moon were illuminated and different types of fireworks lit. At that moment, the ambience resembled a marriage celebration. To heighten the feeling of euphoria, everyone present desired to have a look at the *jogi* who had now assumed the appearance of a bridegroom with gay abandon.

In a nutshell, when it was past midnight, the colours of the world dissipated and the gathering dispersed. The wonder had subsided, feelings were at an ebb. The moon started its journey across the sky and the stars blinked. On opening one's eyes, it was observed that the sky had already changed. Truly, the miracles of this world were transient and time-dependent. None can actually work as per his wish, because a new fancy had accosted him. Consequently, in the month of *saawan*[114], this festival continued to be celebrated and it continued for many years.

Chote Saheb[115]

One day, I was seated in the premises of the *Parikhana*. Chote Khan and Ghulam Raza Khan were present at my service. (Late) Najm un-Nisa Begum and other *paris* were undergoing training in song and dance. All of a sudden, the sky was overcast with clouds and it became dark. In fact, it was so dark that it gave the impression of being night time. This gave goose-bumps to all and fear was palpable. In this backdrop, Ghulam Raza Khan and Chote Khan announced that there lived a woman in Golaganj, who was extremely comely and attractive. But due to the inclement weather, it would not be advisable to leave the safety of the house and venture out. On hearing this, I replied, "It appears that both of you are cowards." At this, both stated, "Please express your wish. We are with you like your own shadow."

At that very moment, I granted permission that the gathering be dispersed. Ghulam Raza Khan, Chote Khan, Najm un-Nisa Begum and few other *paris* remained in my attendance. I entered the palace and re-entered *Parikhana* by way of another entrance. I paused awhile, then attired myself in tight *churidar*[116] and *angrakha*[117]. Taking two pistols, I wrapped a shawl around my body, hiding my face and head. My eyes and eyebrows were partially hidden by the double-layered cap I wore. Fixing a sword at my side, I informed Najm un-Nisa Begum that I was going out, but others should not know about it.

Accompanied by my companions, Ghulam Raza Khan and Chote Khan, I reached the lane outside, by jumping out of a window of *Parikhana*. The dark and deserted lane was truly formidable and we were full of apprehension. Chatting amongst ourselves to dispel our fears, we reached our destination which was known as *kotha*[118] of *Chote Saheb.* I started up the *kotha*, accompanied by my two trusted aides. I had hardly climbed up a few steps to the premises when my arrival was announced. Reaching the top, I observed a reasonably good gathering there. Several youth were present, but they were intimidated by my persona and accoutrements.

The moment we were seated, my confidants gave my introduction as a *Risaldar*[119] from Delhi. Seeing my personality, she immediately became infatuated with me. She sprinkled *itr* on my clothes and offered me a serving of *paan.* Like a crafty, low born person, I removed the *paan* from my mouth, and averting my eyes, handed it over to Chote Khan. Another *paan* was offered to me, which I accepted. After this, I picked up a musical instrument, and started singing the introductory notes of a *ghazal*[120], which had been composed by me in *raag Jhinjhoti*[121]. My music had a devastating effect on that fatal woman. Sobbing, she held my hand and expressed her desire for me. But I behaved nonchalantly, and started petting her cat who was called Moti. I remained indifferent towards her, although her behaviour was ingratiating.

In this manner, the night passed and I conveyed to my companions that we should now be departing. On hearing this, they assisted me in rising. As we were leaving, that beloved became tearful; she arose, removed her costly *dupatta* and wound it around my waist. Then, taking off one of her finger rings, presented it to me, saying, "Although you are now leaving after breaking my heart, you must visit me again and display your talents."

I was still present in the *kotha*, when *thanedar*[122] Umar Khan, announced his arrival in a loud voice. But that woman made an excuse, saying that she had already retired for the night. I descended the stairs and saw the carriage of Baksh Ali Khan. I nimbly hid myself in a doorway of a shop. My companions were a troubled lot. After Baksh Ali Khan had reached some distance, I emerged from the doorway and started walking. On reaching the crossing of Golaganj, I saw that a person, blowing a horn, was approaching me. In those days, it was forbidden to move around, armed with swords, but on seeing my pleasing personality, I was allowed to pass. After all these adventures, I reached *Parikhana* safely. Having traipsed all night in lanes and by bylanes, and because it was still dark, I stretched myself on my bed and went off to sleep. Lowly attendants massaged my feet as I slumbered. The fact of the matter was that due to the strictness of my father, indulging in such daring activities was a challenging task.

A Contest of Good Looks

The building which had been reserved for my companions was

known as *Wazir Manzil*, which was just behind *Shahanshah Manzil*. The martyr's tomb was situated just opposite *Wazir Manzil*. This had been especially embellished and decorated. Once, I was in *Wazir Manzil*. Myself and Chote Khan placed a wager that a contest of our good looks should be held, by inviting a newly appointed woman. In those days, my select companion, Chote Khan, was as alluring as a beautiful statue and as desirable as a lover, being as he was, very proud of his good looks. That night, during a conversation, he said to me, "There are many women who are my admirers, therefore please do not compete with me as far as good looks are concerned. With a mere glance, I can make her my slave. You have unnecessarily thought of having this contest." But I did not heed to his words. I had confidence in myself. Eventually it was decided that the woman who is invited should not be acquainted with either of us, and not seen us before in any gathering or festivity.

After this decision, an extremely attractive and elegant woman was invited. Chote Khan, reposed, with all the finery in dress and accoutrements of a bridegroom. The woman had been invited on the premise that Chote Khan was the owner of the house. When she entered, I hid myself from her presence. As agreed upon, Chote Khan embraced that woman and kissed her. I had previously instructed Chote Khan to completely captivate her and sweep her off her feet. After which, I would make my entrance.

As per plan, the woman in question was completely enamoured by Chote Khan, so much so that Chote Khan was convinced of his victory in the wager. All of a sudden, I appeared in front of them, cloaked in a white sheet and wearing a tall cap. It was night time; I greeted them with an *Assalam va-'laikum*[123]. Chote Khan replied with a *Va-'laikum assalam* and welcomed me with an utterly informal and friendly manner, saying, "Where were you all these days? Come, sit close to me."

I replied, "Since the last several days, I had been intending to meet you, but could not spare time. I shall be in the city for a few days, then return to Shahjahanabad. I have come, only to meet you."

Chote Khan responded, "You have done very well to come here." During this exchange, I observed that the woman, who had been swooning over Chote Khan, increased the flame of the lamp in front of her and started glancing at me. She prepared two spicy *paans* after opening the container, giving one to Chote Khan and offering me the other one, behind his back. I ignored this surreptitious behaviour of hers and continued chatting with Chote Khan, after accepting the *paan.* After this, she started to dig her nails on my feet, behind Chote Khan's back. In a reproachful way, I informed Chote Khan that his woman would defame me with her ardour and he should be strict with her.

On hearing this, she left Chote Khan's side and sat by my side. Chote Khan expressed fake anger, saying, "O rude woman, you have come here on my invitation; what is your concern with another man?"

During this exchange, I picked up the sitar lying there and commenced playing it. She was all praise for me. Things came to such a pass that she threw down the money given to her by Chote Khan, bluntly stating that it was not possible for her to spend the night with him. This infuriated Chote Khan. Ghulam Raza Khan and other attendants had hid themselves nearby. They claimed to have overheard the exchange between the woman and Chote Khan; she had wanted to return to her home, but Chote Khan would not allow her to do so. Eventually, with a lot of difficulty, she agreed to spend the night here, asking me for my address as she wanted to pay me a visit the next night, God willing.

I replied, "I am proceeding to Shahjahanabad tomorrow." After this exchange, I proceeded to my living quarters and went to sleep.

The next day, I came to know that she had spent the night with a lot of difficulty and clearly told Chote Khan that she was not inclined towards him.

Daroga Umrao Begum

After the demise of *daroga* Najm un-Nisa, there was an urgent need for a responsible woman who would take care of all the internal arrangements and requirements. On the recommendation of *daroga* Mir Mohammad Mehdi, this honour was conferred on Umrao Begum. But she could not live up to my expectations.

Daroga Umrao Begum, who was related to Qudsia Mahal, the *begum* of (late) King Nasir-id-Din Haider tried her level best to entice me with her charms, but I did not let her succeed. She would constantly flutter around me like a moth to a flame, and attempt to be intimate with me on some pretext, but each time I would escape from her designs, with a clean slate. Once, she also hinted of a *mut'ah* marriage, but it did not materialise. She performed her duties only superficially; much of the actual work was done by Haji Mohammad Sharif Ali Khan. She was a stout fair woman, thirty five years of age. I never cast any amorous glances towards her.

Mir Mohammad Mehdi and Others are Honoured

With time, Mir Mohammad Mehdi was honoured with the title of Amirul Umr Mir Mohammad Mehdi Sahib. In turn, he appointed Munshi Jafar Ali as his *Naib*[124] and Chote Khan as *daroga* of the fuel (coal) stores. Sheikh Mohammad Baksh was appointed as his assistant. Ghulam Raza Khan was given the charge of caretaker of the premises. Kashi Ram would assist him. Mohammad Moat-mud Ali Khan would be the *daroga* of the *Wali Ahad*'s treasury, who in turn recommended the appointment of Hussain Ali Beg as *daroga* of *Shahanshah Bagh*, *Kasbe Khakan* and *Jahanuma*. Through the good offices of Ali Naqi Khan, Masood Ali Beg was chosen as *daroga* of *Mubaraq Bagh*.

Chote Khan was also given charge of *Khas Makan* (Khas Muqam?). On the other hand, Sabit Ali Khan was given the responsibility of *Makanate Mausuma*, *Razi Manzil*, *Makane Ashiqana Pasand, Makan Mehboob Pasand*, *Qasr-e-Sultan* and others. Mohammad Moat-mud Ali Khan would also take care of

Sikandar Bagh. In reality, this garden surpassed the heavens themselves. Nawab Sikandar Mahal *Saheba* had occupied it during her lifetime. Since she had no heirs, the *bagh* became public property after her demise.

When Ghulam Raza Khan, Sabit Ali Khan and Kashi Ram were given charge of developing *Sikandar Bagh*. Due to simultaneous work being carried out by several people, the building could be finished in one year's time. Otherwise, even seven to eight years would not have been sufficient. A sum of rupees five lakhs were spent on its building, but it set a precedent for others. A majestic mosque was built in the centre, which could be seen from outside. The gateway leading to the complex was so magnificent that something like this was not present in the heaven's themselves. A path led from the garden to the river. A person standing on the balcony of the building could observe the river from afar. The pathway was lined with fruit bearing trees on either side. And it was so wide that three carriages could pass through side-by-side, and yet some space would be available on both sides[125].

Rahas Leela

On one auspicious day (with the usual epithets), the whole of *Huzur Bagh* was decked up with flowers. I graced the premises, with all the paraphernalia required for music and dance. At that moment, I directed the *paris* to engage in *Rahas Leela*[126]. This is a dance form considered holy by the Hindus, who spend vast sums of money on this form of worship, through dance. It depicts Kanhaiya (Lord Krishna) and his *gopis*[127]. It is not a false rumour that the dance form which I had produced had no parallel elsewhere. Various *paris* had been trained with great effort by maestros. Actually, seven people in my employ had been responsible for giving this craft its final shape. The play actors were as follows:

- Sultan Pari: Radha, Kanhaiya's favourite *gopi*
- Marukh: Kanhaiya
- Yasmin Pari, Dilruba Pari, Hur Pari: Other *gopis*

Considerable amount of money had to be spent on arranging this play. Other than the appurtenances, a sum of rupees five hundred had been spent on general arrangements. To detail the expenses of the *pooja*[128] items, together with garments, decorations, etc. would be an exercise in futility. The devotees of Kanhaiya, expressing divine love, were known as *gopis*. This dance form had roots in Hindustani music, expressing union and separation (of the spirit). This dance form is performed only in the evenings, after sunset. When its preparations and arrangements were complete, I invited my younger brother, Mirza Sikandar Hashmat to participate in the event. He accepted by invitation with alacrity and participated whole-heartedly in the occasion. The *paris* had adorned and perfumed themselves for this festivity. They were seated on chairs, all around me, with great poise and style. This event, comprising of song and drama, was so superlative that each and every person could do nothing except applaud. My brother was seated beside me, blooming like a flower. Lights made of glass twinkled everywhere. The throne was covered from all sides with flowers, like bedspreads. Special screens had been arranged for those in *purdah* (veiled), and they enjoyed the sight from behind these screens. This life-giving company finally dispersed after midnight. Guests returned to their homes and I went off to sleep.

A Fair

The *paris* had a boundless desire for a *Meena Bazar* and Fair to be organised. Accordingly, I ordered that a *Meena Bazar*-cum-Fair should take place. Immediately after getting the order, craftsmen and professionals presented their goods. Stalls were put up with a lot of finesse and competence. Whoever partook of a sweetmeat from a stall, experienced the pleasure of eating all kinds of sweetmeats from across the world. A vegetable seller had arranged his wares in baskets of every conceivable colour. Apples, peaches, pears and dry fruits such as pistachios and almonds had been presented beautifully, the latter bearing resemblance to a lovers' lips and eyes.

One woman was causing admirers to swoon over her unusual, coquettish overtures. Smokers of cannabis and tobacco, were exhaling intoxicating smoke into the atmosphere. Stalls selling *kebabs*[129] gave consolation to the heart-broken. Broken hearts were being tortured. Every *kebab* would literally be the envy of chicken and fish (dishes, due to the demand). Lime juice and ginger created their own magic on this dish.

The reddish mouths of beauteous maidens were being enhanced by the sellers of *paan*. Aroma of kebabs and *sheermal*[130] prepared by *naanbais*[131] permeated the air, bringing succor to the mind. There was a long queue outside the stalls of flower-sellers; every stall displayed a wide variety of flowers. Like the songs of nightingales, the liveliness of the flower sellers filled the hearts of the alluring ladies with longing.

Toys made of mica and burnt clay were successfully competing with porcelain of Chinese origin. Performers and artists displayed their skills and artistry with sprightliness. In one corner, a fight between a snake and a mongoose was in progress. Both were entwined with each other, with complete lack of fear. The weakened creature would have it's head scraped on the ground by its foe, scaring spectators witnessing the show. A large gathering was present at the site, and the fate of the creatures was in the hands of God.

In one area, there was a large collection of trunks, containing more trunks inside. Like a magical show, some feathers had been kept in the trunks, and the magician would convert these feathers to pigeons to the awe of the spectators. This display caused a large crowd to gather. Folk dancers exhibited their talents everywhere. They had a kinship with Iran and enjoyed self-esteem there, but in India, were looked down upon, as they belonged to the lower strata of society. Several artists were required to put up a display; one would beat the drum, while others would draw the attention of the audience with different actions and gestures. It was generally accepted that the beating of the drum had some kind of mesmerizing effect, as a result of which people were hypnotized. One person would climb on an upright spear with the help of a rope; another would walk on a naked sword and perform other acrobatics.

In this performance, artists would dismember themselves then become bodily whole again. They would claim that they had the ability to make an old man young once again, to transform a human being into a demon, and also to reincarnate the dead. They could sow seeds and grow trees, and also harvest flowers and fruits from those trees. Some young men of this group were chatting among themselves, and the women were displaying their bodies.

In one place, a gathering of story tellers were regaling the public with their stories. Their intention was to pocket the money belonging to the audience. The spectators were generally bewildered and astonished, while those adept in all this were whispering amongst themselves. Games of *chausar*[132] and chess were also in progress. Some people were arguing and fighting among themselves, declaring themselves as *Wazir*. It was s strange sight to behold. A poor man could become rich in a few moments, and a rich man could become a pauper in a matter of minutes. This absurd game was the cause of much exploitation of the poor by the rich; the former would slide into the pit of destruction and subjugation. But corrupt officers were hand-in-glove with the perpetrators and preferred to turn their eyes away from all this exploitation.

Although the king's belief in the *Sharia* was enough to keep the situation under control, yet the presence of corrupt, shameless, and uncontrollable officers and religious leaders resulted in these sort of offences being committed. These people would literally encourage crime and animal-like tendencies, devoting their lives to devilry, intoxication and drunkenness.

The same condition could be seen with drunkards and opium eaters. When they were among people of their own ilk, they would simply forget good sense and decency, being unaware of the world. One fellow was yawning prodigiously after snorting from a *chillum*[133], while another was totally naked and whirling like those who dance to *qawwalis*[134] in *mazars*[135]. Sometimes, he would giggle and laugh, akin to the sound of liquor being poured into a *surahi*[136]. Sometimes he would weep, the sound resembling the call of a mynah bird. In short, everyone was intoxicated with the intoxicant of his choice. These intoxicants were in cooked form, some ground and some dripping. These shameless people had no regret or embarrassment at their behaviour which was totally against decency and social norms. A lion had been brought to this fair, which sucked milk from the udders of a goat. The public were amazed at this sight of an impossibility becoming a possibility.

I had provided the *kaharins*[86] present with an ample amount of money and expensive clothes (with gold weave). These gorgeous females frolicked among the crowds, engaged in coquetry and merriment. The crowds present, amazed at this sight, loudly exclaimed their helplessness before these seductive creatures.

My regal persona, seated on an elephant, was moved slowly through the crowd, casting coins among the public with both hands. I cast my benevolent shadow on each and everyone present, all the while keenly noting the various objects of interest in the fair. *Fakirs* and the indigent were fully provided for with means and government officials were instructed to buy all the goods from the sellers at ten times their cost, so that all of them would become rich, and this generosity would serve as an example for the world.

All these purchased goods were sent to my honourable father, the king, as a tribute. Exhibiting his fatherly love, he graciously accepted the gifts, stating that the entire Meena Bazar had been purchased, but he had been kept in dark about it. Anyway, what was done was appreciable, but he should be kept informed in future.

Jashn-e-Mahtabi

Kings have traditionally made full arrangements for the training of their female companions, resulting in the latter becoming highly trained in the arts and crafts. Notable among them have been

Mohammad Shah[137], King of Delhi, the Sultan of Bijapur, Adil Shah[138] and other rulers, who trained beautiful and elegant women in music, raising their status as formal singers.

Accordingly, this royal personage, following tradition, also arranged for the musical upbringing and schooling of several beautiful women, whose mere gestures could act like arrows, proving fatal for prospective lovers. The ribbons used to braid their hair resembled black serpents. Eyebrows were poisonous scorpions, ready to strike. Their singing was indeed divine. The soul would struggle to free itself from the body. On witnessing a dance performance, even a fire-worshipper would bow his head and prostate himself in reverence. The audience would be amazed on seeing the flashy and gorgeous dresses and beautiful ornaments. The planets would forget their orbits and plead to learn the nuances of dance of *Indrasabha*. Peacocks would become attendants. Just as day and night have a thousand nuances, these dancing girls too would exhibit novel dance forms, new musical compositions and contemporary styles, which gave succour to the soul. Arms would flutter like a fish out of water. Soon after I had given orders that their musical training should be completed in all respects, these *paris* attained such perfection and became such adepts, that one could consider them worthy of competing with maestros such as Tansen[139] and Baiju[140].

It was the fourteenth day of the (Islamic) month[141]. The moon was in the peak of its splendour and glory. I summoned all those who had become adept, informing them that all kinds of delicious food items would be provided as per their choice, and they should make arrangements for whatever was required by them. On hearing my orders, the entire group of artists gathered near the *Dar-e-Daulat*[142]. When the gathering was complete, and the event commenced, each and every gorgeous female dancer, their bodies shimmering like silver, displayed her talents with song and dance, suffusing the universe with their essence. No one could gather courage to criticize or point their finger at these divine beings personifying the glorious moon. Among all of them, Sultan Pari excelled to such an extent with the display of her talents that I fell in love with her. The spectators, well versed in the nuances of music declared in a single voice that this was not music but a miracle.

Karim Baksh Amir Baksh Wali

One day, while the sky was overcast with dark clouds and I was enjoying the pleasures of song and dance, a woman made an entrance in the gathering. She had been previously employed as a singer in the court of late Nasir-ud-Din Haider, and after his demise, had adopted prostitution as a profession. She was around thirty five years of age. Initially she developed contacts with Amman, and after a lot of effort on her part, she reached me one dark rainy night, accompanied by Ghulam Raza Khan and Chote Khan. I admitted her to the court, but due to her advanced age, did not develop any relations with her. However, I did provide her with gifts and clothes worth rupees two thousand. Albeit I did not feel like parting from her, yet I bid her farewell, following the old adage in Hindi that one can clap with both hands only.

After a few days, I developed a dalliance with Pyari Umda Khanum. She had a squint in her eyes and was known by this name only. I wasted several thousands of rupees on her, but ultimately broke away due to her squint.

Subsequently, I had a romantic relationship with Bano Farqanda Wali. She too had been an attendant of the singers in the court of Nasir-ud-Din Haider. She was also infatuated with me. For a whole year, she did not leave my household, but due to her advanced age, I had to bid her farewell. She was very upset at this, and kept weeping at our separation. She had remained as a companion of one of my *begums*, and continued to send pleas for joining my household, but I remained aloof. Ultimately she entered into a *mut'ah*[84] marriage with Mohammad Raza Khan.

In a similar manner, a woman named Gauhar became enamoured with me, keeping alive her hopes of a union for a full year. We would exchange love notes through the medium of Ghulam Raza. But due to reasons unknown, our meeting could not materialise. Before this, a lady from Hussainabad, who was devoid of any proficiency in music, had been ignored by me.

Umrao Choti Khanum also came in my presence, but I could not love her as I had been unwell at that time.

A maidservant named Kanhaiya was also captivated with me, but I did not accept her. Out of desperation, she entered the household of *daroga* Ahmed Ali and continues to live there.

A prostitute called Bakshi, who was highly unattractive and coarse was also unable to join my household.

Chapla Bi provided her services to me for a single night only. Bandi Habshin Wali, who was a slave and lover of *naib daroga* Haider Hussain Khan, made her appearance in my presence one day but I bid her farewell. I believe that she continues to remain in touch with Haider Hussain Khan. For quite some time, she continued to pine for me, but I refused to accept her. Dejected, she eventually entered someone's household[144].

After this, a woman named Ali Jaan expressed her desire for my attentions. She would express her intentions by way of gestures during song and dance performance, in full view of others in the gatherings. Sometimes, she would hold my hand, and on other occasions, she would wear charms, containing my musical and poetical compositions. Sometimes, she would complain, sometimes sigh and sometimes send me messages, expressing her desire to join my troupe of *paris*. Because of this reason, I had some inclination towards her and desired that I should accommodate her on some pretext.

In those days, I had learnt about a dispute pending in the *Sharia* court involving Karim Baksh and Amir Baksh, her aggrieved mother. Karim Baksh was involved with an Agha Hasan. Mir Ali Hussain was the deputy of *daroga* Mir Mohammad Mehdi and handled all the day-to-day work of the latter. Agha Hasan was the brother of this very Mir Ali Hussain.

Mohammad Moat-mud Ali Khan was very keen to gather singing and dancing women and present them before me. He was interested in getting this dispute of Karim Baksh -Amir Baksh being disposed off and Karim Baksh be inducted in my establishment, after freeing her from the clutches of Agha Hasan. Sabit Ali Khan also entertained similar ideas, in another matter. I had instructed both that the legal disputes of these women should be dealt with in some way and that they should be brought to my presence.

Ali Jaan was in love with a soldier, and did not agree to this proposition. I was amazed that this very woman had expressed her love for me, and had wanted to join my household, then after all, what in Allah's name could be the matter? Then I consoled my self with the thought that the matter would be resolved when she appeared before me.

Because she had been imprisoned for being intoxicated, there was no simple way that she could have been freed. God willing, I would include her in my retinue, after I assumed my rightful place on the royal seat.

I sent secret messages to Karim Baksh through Sheikh Hussain Ali and Chote Khan, as a result of which she became infatuated with me. Subsequently, I summoned Agha Hasan and tried my best to convince him. However, that fraudster agreed to my proposals in my presence, but petitioned my father behind my back, accusing me of coercion and manhandling. As a result of this, the following order were sent to the jail staff :

"*It is possible that a representative of the Crown Prince may try to influence the proceedings of the case. No heed is to be taken to this, and Karim Baksh should be handed over to Amir Baksh.*"

The orders were implemented accordingly. Amir Baksh was given the custody of her daughter, Karim Baksh. I tried to convince Karim Baksh for a month, that her mother (Amir Baksh) was not fit to retain her custody and that she was a mortal enemy (of her own daughter). After sustained effort, she agreed to join my household, and Agha Hasan was proved wrong. But that brainless Amir Baksh refused to cooperate, which hurt my sentiments considerably.

When Karim Baksh joined her mother after being freed from imprisonment, she did not meet Agha Hasan. I came to know that Agha Hasan consumed four to five *tolas* of opium out of sheer humiliation. But due to his sturdy constitution, he remains alive to this day.

By approaching people holding important posts in the government through Sabit Ali and Mohammad Moat-mud Ali Khan, I tried my level best to influence the case of Ali Jaan and Karim Baksh. But I could not achieve any success. I bribed Agha Mohammad, a staff of the jail, with five hundred rupees. He accepted the money but did not act according to my wishes. I cannot narrate just how much the staff of the jailhouse confounded me. I sent letters to several people, but that did not solve any purpose. But they cast a smear on my heart. Thousands of rupees were wasted on the staff of the jailhouse and *Sharia* department, but I could not succeed in achieving my goal. I was helpless due to fear of my esteemed father. I could only hope that God, in his greatness, would show the path by which this curtain of separation would be cast aside.

Bandi Umda Wali

It was the auspicious month of *Ramzān*[141]. I had partaken of the *sehri*[146] and was about to sleep when Mohammad Moat-mud Ali Khan kneaded my back. I exclaimed in surprise, "Why are you taking this trouble at this hour?" He replied, "A woman by the name of Bandi Umda Wali has expressed her infatuation for you, and is presently sitting on the terrace of this building." Because I had my eyes on her for some time, I immediately proceeded to the terrace. She was actually sitting here. On seeing me, she got up from her seat, and running up to me, embraced me. I asked about her well-being, and she replied, "I have managed to come here on the pretext of a dance performance. If my mother comes to know, she will be furious." I queried as to how we could meet in the future? She replied, "Let *Muharram* be over. After that, I shall come myself." After that day, my love for her was like an arrow piercing my heart. I prayed that this separation be over. During this period, I had the opportunity to meet her a few times. But due to circumstances beyond my control, I could not induct her in my household.

Amir Baksh

Through one of my courtiers, a prostitute by the name of Amir Baksh joined as my attendant and became enamoured with me. She was accommodated in a room in *Huzur Bagh*. I arranged for her comforts through Chote Khan. I would frequently visit her in her room. There would be sessions of song and music also. This incensed the *paris* and they set up a clamour; Mashuq-e-Khas engineered a forceful protest over this. Other than all this, the woman also suffered from a dangerous ailment, as a result of which, I abstained from meeting her.

Decoration of a Cultural Gathering

One day, I arranged a cultural gathering in a venue where lush trees swayed joyously in the breeze, and peacocks were responding to this in ecstasy. European lanterns lit up every corner of *Huzur Bagh* and *Shahanshah Bagh*. Sitting arrangements had been made in the royal palace. The *paris* were busy displaying their talents. Singers with melodious voices, possessing the anguish and restlessness of flames were engaged in crooning their mellifluous compositions. On this occasion, I awarded Rashq Pari with the honorific title of Malka-e-Mahe Alam Mashuq-e-Khanum Shahzadi

Saheba. Shahanshah Pari was given the title of Mushfiq-e-Jahani Husn Ara Nawab Shahanshah Begum Saheba, Sardar Pari was honoured as Shafiq-tul-Zamani Mallika Sardar Begum Saheba, Sarfaraz Pari as Ashiqan-e-Khas Anjuman-e-Afroz Sarfaraz Begum Saheba, Sikandar Begum Saheba as Habibtul Sultan Makarmatul Zamani Sikandar Begum Saheba, Dildar Pari as Bazm-e-Afroz Dilruba Pari, Amir Pari as Khurshidulqa Amir Pari and Hur Pari as Jane Jahan Hur Begum. Other *paris* continued to retain their original titles. Each *pari* was provided with individual accommodation and every *begum* was provided with four menservants and expensive gold parasols to enhance their status. I was enamoured with Mashuq-e-Khas and spent a lot of money on her. Due to this reason, she also gifted me with many costly garments.

I was always indebted to Mashuq-e-Khas. A piece of estate, which my father had gifted me a long time ago was also transferred to her. I also gifted her with landed property and riches, details of which would become too lengthy and tedious.

In those days, I appointed a *Maulvi* named Mirza Hasan, and allotted a portion of the palace to him for setting up a seminary. Every *begum* attended and acquired knowledge of Islamic education, which continued till I ascended the throne.

In those days, Sarfarazo had been appointed in my establishment on a pay of rupees five hundred. This was the same Sarfarazo, whose resemblance to Nanhi Begum I had described previously. She continued in her job till the death of my father, and my ascension to the throne.

Death of Amjad Ali Shah

I felt surrounded with immense sorrow, as if I had been enveloped in darkness, when my esteemed father died. Lucknow, a bed of roses, which could put the heavenly gardens to shame appeared to have become a garden of stone. The bird of contentment, which resided in the hearts of the people, seemed to have flown away somewhere. Palaces and harems became deserted and desolate. Tears resembling pearls could be seen in a thousand eyes. Sorrow knocked on every breast. The vapours from collective sighs created another sky below the normal one. The flood of tears reminded one of the flood which had occurred during the times of Noah. Especially this human being, who had loved his father dearly, was unable to bear the sorrow of his demise.

But the Maker of this world perhaps desired that the garden of Lucknow to bloom again, and the glory of the royal throne to attain its splendour once again. At that time, I was heartbroken over the demise of my father, and my grief threatened to fragment my heart to pieces. The night was still not over, when a messenger from the British Resident appeared and invited me to accompany him on horseback[147]. In that hour of morning, I was obliged to follow him on horseback. It was a strange moment. My devoted followers surrounded the horse near the *Dar-e-Daulat.* I entered *Gulistan-e-Iram*[148] and had a discussion with the Resident, on the question of how my later father was to be honoured. I replied that *Jannat Makān*[149] would be the apt title for him considering our lineage.

The Coronation

After this meeting, I proceeded to the upper story of the palace, offered prayers of thanksgiving, after which, I was crowned by imperial *Mujtahid-ul*[150]. Following this, lead a procession to the throne, where I was presented with *nazar*[151] by the nobles and the dignitaries of the court. Cannons boomed in salutation, and I was seated on the throne for some time.

Because I was overwhelmed with grief, and my tears would not stop, I went to the palace behind the *baradari*, and rested for awhile. That night, the company of *paris* and companions was not available. Through Mohammad Moat-mud Khan, I made a bracelet from the finger rings obtained from each *pari* and *begum*, and wore it around my neck.

The next day, I gifted my courtiers and followers with swords, honours and appropriate titles. In those days, Ustad Amin-ud-Daula

Bahadur[153] was the Prime Minister, and I wanted to give this post to Ali Naqi Khan. Due to this reason, the former was not given any honours. The titles which were conferred on that day are as follows:

- Ghulam Raza Khan: Sabit-ud-Daula Bahadur
- Ghulam Yadullah Khan: Qutub-ud-Daula Mufta-hul-Mulk Munise Dil Pazeer
- Mohammad Qutub Ali Khan Bahadur: Kayam Jung Bahadur Musahib-e-Khas Hazrat Sultané Alam Khulullah Mulk-e-Sultané

It should be noted that every title would be compulsorily suffixed by the term, "Musahib-e-Khas Hazrat Sultané Alam. In the same way, Sheikh Ghulam Ali Bahadur-ud-daula, Mir Akbar Ali, the present *Naib* (deputy) of Mahasul Sultan, was conferred the title of Akbar-ud-Daula. Others were given honoured as per their posts and abilities. *Khwajasārās*[42] were also honoured appropriately:

- Mohammad Moat-mud Ali Khan: Dayanat-ud-Daula Mulk
- Mohammad Bashir Ali Khan: Mubashirul Mulk
- Mohammad Rehan Ali Khan: Gulbadan-ud-Daula Mulk Mohammad Rehan Ali Khan Sabt Jung

During my days as *Wali Ahad*, another *khwajasārā* of Abyssinian origin had been appointed through Dayanat-ud-Daula. He was given the permanent title of Ahsan-ud-Daula Mohsin-ul-Mulk. Other *khwajasārās* were also awarded permanent titles. Haji Mohammad Hilal Ali Khan, a highly accomplished, intelligent gentleman, who was fluent in Arabic and *Farsi* (Persian) was given the title of Zair-ud-Daula. Najad *khwajasārā*, another Abyssinian, from the days when I was Crown Prince, who had come from the household of Nawab Suleiman Mahal Saheba, was awarded the title of Mubaraq-ud-Daula Khurd. Mazi-ud-Daula was given the charge of *Ghanghor* platoon. This platoon, known as *Risala Bodyguard* had four hundred British horsemen. Afsar-ud-Daula

Bahadur was given the responsibility of the Nagaria and Balak Ganj Artilleries. A relative of Razi-ud-Daula, *bhai* Ghulam Hasan Khan was given the title of Wahid-ud-Daula and given the responsibility of *Khan-e-Sultani*, *daroga* of the *Doab*[154]. Wahaj-ud-Daula was given the charge of the Royal Magazine and Sabit-ud-Daula was made In Charge of the Treasury.

Qutub-ud-Daula was given the responsibility of the Royal offices. Feroz *khwajasārā* was awarded the title of Feroz-ud-Daula Bahadur and appointed as supervisor of pensions and grants of *begums* and pensioners. Bashir-ud-Daula was given the responsibility of serving *Khas Mahal.* Moat-mud Ali Khan was given a fresh set of responsibilities. Bahadur-ud-Daula Bahadur was made the *daroga* of *Bharmar Paltan* (platoon). A temporary courtier, Musammi Bhura was given the permanent title of Aijaz-ud-Daula. Gulbadan-ud-Daula Bahadur was given the responsibility of *Rwan-e-Khas Sultani*. Mubaraq-ud-Daula was made responsible for the upkeep of *Najaf Shareef* (*Shahnajaf*) and Maqbara of Nasir-ud-Din Haider. A sum of ten lakh rupees was allotted from the Royal Treasury, towards the Maqbara of *Jannat Makan* (late Amjad Ali Shah), for which Ghulam Ali Khan Ibn-e-Ghulam Raza, who had been awarded the title of Najib-ud-Daula Bahadur, was made responsible, and who would be assisted by Bashir-ud-Daula.

Sheikh Mohammad Baksh, who had been In-charge of the coal bin as deputy of Anis-ud-daula continued in his post, and subsequently promoted as *Naayak*[155] of the fully modernised platoon of British soldiers.

The title of Musharaf-ud-Daula-Sharif-ud-Daula Jaan-Nisaar[156]-e-Sarkar Hazrat Sultan-e-Alam Khuld-Ullah Karnail[157] Haji Mohammad Sharif Sharafat Jang was given to Jaan-Nisaar Huzoor Wali Ahmed Bahadur Karnail Haji Mohammad Sharif Ali Khan. Aijaz Baksh was appointed as officer of the horsemen, known as Body Guard. He had been looking after the entire affairs of the Home Department, during my days as Crown Prince and his charge remained the same. After some time, Amin-ud-Daula desired to be relieved due to his health condition and was replaced by Ali Naqi Khan, who had started his career in Faizabad with the title of Madar-ud-Daula Bahadur, ultimately becoming the Prime Minister (of the kingdom).

Award of the Title of *Mahal* to *Begums* and *Paris*

The habits, interests, faithfulness as well as perfidy of various *begums*, *paris* and lovers had been well known to me, from my days as the crown prince. After ascending the royal seat as king, it was no longer feasible to keep these under cover. Hence, I resolved to keep them confined (in my harem) after enticing them with money. However, the unreliable among these women, who were on the lookout to escape were not given this opportunity. Eventually, one day, I confined the various *paris*, after giving them titles as below:

- The title of Malika-e-Mahe Alam Mashuq-e-Khas Hazrat Sultan-e-Alam Sultanat Mahal Saheba was bestowed upon Mashuq-e-Khas
- Sarfaraz Begum was given the title of Ashiq-e-Khas Anjuman-e-Afroz Nawab Sarfaraz Mahal Saheba
- Sardar Begum was honoured by the title of Shafiq-ul-Zamani Banki Jaan Nawab Sardar Mahal Saheba
- Bazm-e-Afroz Dilruba Begum was conferred the title of Bazm-e-Afroz Nawab Dilruba Mahal Saheba
- Khurshid-ul-Ka Amir Begum was given the title of Khurshid-ul-Ka Nawab Amir Mahal Saheba
- Jaan-e-Jahan Hur Begum was honoured as Nawab Hur Mahal Saheba
- Sultan Pari was honoured as Nawab Sultan Jahan Mahal Saheba
- Yasmin Pari was given the title of Nawab Yasmin Mahal Saheba

- Huzoor Pari was named Nawab Huzoor Mahal Saheba
- Sikandar Begum was honoured by the title of Habibul Sultan Mukarram Tuzzma Nawab Sikandar Mahal Saheba
- Wazir Pari was named as Nawab Khurshid Mahal Saheba
- Nawab Mashuq Mahal Saheba was honoured by the title of Meher-tan-Afsar-un-Nisa Nawab Nishat Mahal Nanhi Begum Saheba
- Nawab Izzat Mahal Saheba was given the title of Mallika-e-Parivash Nawab Sultan Mahal Saheba
- Iftikhar-un-Nisa Khanum Saheba was honoured as Nawab Hazrat Mahal Saheba
- Umrao Khanum was named as Nawab Umrao Mahal Saheba
- Ajaib Pari was honoured as Ajaib Khanum Saheba
- Badshah Baksh was renamed as Rahatul Sultan
- Shirin Habshin was honoured as Aramul Sultan
- Mahrukh Pari was given the title of Mahrukh Begum Saheba
- Laila Habshin was honoured as Muti-ul-Sultan
- Ambar Afshaan Habshin was honoured as Hafiz-ul-Sultan

Haidri Begum, had been removed from the harem, when I had been Crown Prince, on the charge of having consumed ground glass, but had been reinstated shortly afterwards through the grace of Qutub-ud-Din Bahadur. She was honoured by the title of Sayyid-un-Nisa Haidri Begum Saheba

Shahanshah Mahal Saheba, Dildar Mahal Saheba, Sikandar Mahal Saheba, Sarfaraz Mahal Saheba and Sardar Mahal Saheba were further awarded a monthly grant of rupees three thousand. Others were granted a sum of rupees two thousand per month.

Nawab Khas Mahal was honoured by the title of Malik-e-Muqqadar-e-Uzma Nawab Badhshah Mahal Saheba, with a monthly grant of rupees five thousand. Similarly, the princes were also granted titles and awarded monthly stipends.

After some time, currency notes worth lakhs of rupees were given to all those working in the palace, including attendants, courtiers and eunuchs, simply to encourage them.

Habibtul Sultan was similarly honoured. Mirza Falak Qadr Bahadur was elevated to the rank of Crown Prince, and Mirza Kaiwan Qadr Bahadur was given the post of General of the Imperial forces[30]. It may be noted that these two were foster brothers.

Ali Jaan Mangi Wali

Two months after my coronation, I continued to weep bitterly over the elevation of those *begums* and *paris* who had been elevated to the status of *mahals*[24]. Even momentary peace evaded me, but I was helpless. What could I have done in such circumstances? Eventually, a plan formed in my mind, which I tried to implement. The cases of two women were pending in the Appeals Department. One was Karim Baksh, who genuinely loved me. She had been entangled in the ringlets of my hair, right from my days as Crown Prince. The other woman was Ali Jaan. The latter was angry at me, and the reason for this could be ascertained only when she was physically brought in my presence. Amir Baksh, the mother of Karim Baksh was summoned, and with her consent, Karim Baksh was inducted in my household. The title of Bashir-ul-Sultan Gulzar Begum Saheba was conferred upon her.

When Ali Jaan was summoned, she raised heaven and earth by weeping her eyes out. Eventually, I asked her, "What is the reason behind this crying of yours?" She responded, "I still love that soldier." On hearing this, I summoned the soldier to my court the next day and handed over the custody of Ali Jaan to him. He returned to his home after wishing me good tidings.

Honouring of Courtiers

In those days, I conferred honours to the junior courtiers too, and promoted to higher posts. Ghaseeta Khan was given the title of Musahib-ud-Daula Bahadur, giving him the responsibility of conveying petitions to the king. Mohammad Hasan was named Muti-ud-Daula Khan Bahadur, Khwaja Baksh Khan Biradar Qutub-d-Daula Bahadur as Razi-ud-Daula Bahadur and Ghulam Nabi Khan Razi-ud-Daula's paternal uncle, Ghulam Nabi Khan as Tahseen-ud-Daula. Razi-ud-Daula's uncle was given the honorific title of Nisha-ud-Daula Ghulam Haider Khan Bahadur, and those connected with music and dance were made *darogas*. The title of Mustaqim-ud-Daula was given to Alhaiyya Khan, together with the responsibility of In-Charge, Royal Stores. Nisar Ali Khan and Haider Ali Khan were deprived of any honours as they had failed to serve satisfactorily; however, I remained concerned about them.

Sixteen Courtesans

During this period, I suffered from palpitations of the heart. The confinement of the *begums* and *mahals* behind the veil was proving intolerable. Consequently, few dancing girls were appointed as maidservants. Among them, Bandi Umda Wali was the best. These women had once met me at *Jahanuma* palace, when I had been Crown Prince. A total of sixteen women were thus appointed in this manner. However, they were incapable of serving me in the manner similar to the service the mothers of my children had earlier provided, before getting the title of *mahal.*

During my days as Crown Prince, I had a special place in my heart for Bandi. For this reason, I arranged for a buggy to take her to *Huzur Bagh* for her leisure and also presented her with gold and jewellery. Although I was interested in Hasan Bandi and Chuttan also, but I was more inclined towards Bandi (Umda). With time, the friendship between these two women (Hasan and Chuttan) blossomed, as a result of which, Bandi (Umda) was consumed with jealousy. I realised that due to this rivalry, it was possible that the two women would leave my company, and hence, after hesitating for quite some time, extending a loving gesture to Chuttan and Hasan. I knew that these women were as frisky as scampering deer. But I managed to bridle them, as a result of which they remained in my establishment. One was given the title of Mushqul Sultan Khusro Saheba and the other as Nawab Ashiqul Sultan Kaiser Begum Saheba, with a remuneration of rupees two thousand per month.

Umda Bandi Wali

When I was free from the affairs of Khusro Begum and Kaiser Begum, I turned my attentions towards Umda. However, by this time, she had been consumed by the fires of envy. After due counsel with my courtiers, she was given the title of Matlubul Sultan Hazrat Begum Saheba, with a monthly remuneration of two thousand, five hundred rupees, and inducted in my household.

Umrao Begum

In those days, a professional courtesan called Ramzan was brought in my presence through Razi-ud-Daula Bahadur. I accepted her and inducted her in my establishment, together with her mother. She was given the title of Huzrul Sultan Umrao Begum Saheba, on a monthly wage of rupees two thousand. It was a fact that this woman was outstanding in singing and dancing.

Badshah Begum

In those days, another woman caught my fancy, and was accepted in my household through Razi-ud-Daula Bahadur. She was given the title of Mehboob Sultan Badshah Begum Saheba.

Imtiaz Begum

A woman called Imtiaz became enamoured with me. She was also inducted through Razi-ud-Daula Sahib. She was given the title of Imtiaz Begum.

Negligence of Safaraz Mahal

Soon after Sarfaraz was honoured with the title of *mahal*, her movements became restricted in the palace and I also became engrossed with the other recently added *begums*. I came to know that she was not adhering to the traditions associated with the *purdah* (veil). She would gaze at the sight of the Gomti from the premises of the *Chattar Manzil* (palace). Nawab Khurd Mahal Umda Begum Saheba also informed that Sarfaraz Mahal would weep due to her confinement behind the veil.

When Sarfaraz Mahal happened to meet me, she would tell me that it was her separation from me, that made her weep. At this, I would say that I was unable to solve this problem (rigours of the purdah causing this agony to her). Once or twice, I observed her inappropriate actions myself, and on being questioned, she swore otherwise. She wanted that either I should be with her, or else, she should be allowed to move outside.

I explained to her in different ways that after confinement behind the *purdah*, it was very inappropriate to venture outside. But she refused to listen, and continued to weep uncontrollably. Sometimes, she would not take her meals for days, and on other occasions, would clutch at me and not let go of me. She would also threaten me that she would commit suicide, if I did not take her out.

On the other hand, Nawab Sultanat Mahal Saheba also swore on my head that if Sarfaraz Mahal was allowed to step outside, then she would also fearlessly follow suit. Actually, Sultanat Saheba was unable to bear the sorrow of parting from me, and within a period of one year and few months, she appeared to be an invalid of many years. She neither had any agility nor any beauty or attractiveness of youth. I would often ask about her welfare, but it was as if her lips were sealed and she never spoke anything. But her appearance indicated the agony of her separation from me. Nevertheless, I prevented her from thinking thoughts of moving outside by way of different and varied excuses and reasons.

Demise of Mahrukh

The savage news regarding the death of Mahrukh reached my

ears. My heart was wrenched to pieces on hearing this news. This fatal development made me uncontrollable with grief and I sobbed loudly, after collapsing on my bed. But other than having patience, there was no other option. May Allah grant her a place in heaven.

Another Reason for Sorrow

The sad news of the demise of Zaib-un-Nisa Khanum Saheba, the mother of Princess Jahanara Begum Saheba was conveyed to me. At that time, Princess Jahanara Begum was merely six months old. The deceased had been a patient of tuberculosis. I was highly disturbed and gave the custody of the child to her grandmother, i.e. my mother[158]. With the Grace of God, she is growing up well in the loving care of her grandmother. May God grant her long life.

Badshah Bagh and Sarfaraz Mahal

A cool breeze was blowing one day. Singers were creating magic with their mellifluous songs. All of a sudden, I felt like visiting *Badshah Bagh*. Impatiently, I ordered all the *mahals* to proceed, except Sarfaraz, whom I prohibited from going. The *mahals, wazirs, amirs* and others mounted horses and accompanied me, relaxing for few days there. I came to know that on that very night, Sarfaraz Mahal removed a diamond from a ring and swallowed it. This perturbed me so much that I swooned and fell down. Summoning Bashir-ud-Daula, I exclaimed, "Ah! My heart has become so feeble that it no longer has the strength to withstand such sad news."

Many people counselled me to be patient. I continued to grieve in the presence of my mother. A line of attendants had been put on duty from *Badshah Bagh* to *Chattar Manzil*, to give me a minute-by-minute account of developments. The entire atmosphere of leisure and joy had been dispersed like the pouring of sand or the scattering of leaves during autumn. Eventually, after hastening in every possible manner, I reached *Badshah Manzil* from *Badshah*

Bagh. Thankfully, no sad incident occurred. By the Grace of God, Sarfaraz's health improved.

She would always implore me to keep her by my side. Eventually, the bearers of good news conveyed to me that Sarfaraz was expecting. I thanked the Almighty for his benevolence and loved her even more than ever. After that, I would take her out on rides with me every day. But perhaps the Almighty had other plans. After a period of five months, I was informed that Sarfaraz had suffered a miscarriage. I mourned at this and prayed for her good health.

Eventually my prayers bore fruit. But Nawab Saltanat Mahal and Nawab Sarfaraz Mahal continued to pester me on the issue of going out. Moreover, as in previous times, disturbing news of the conduct of these two started reaching my ears. Finally, I addressed my heart thus, "O innocent, when the very intent of confining her behind the veil is not getting achieved, what would be the purpose of confining her thus as *mahal*?" Accordingly, one day, I held hands of both and tried to reason with them, "God has given you this honour of reaching my palace as *mahal* and how you want to participate in the festivities outside with Kaiser Begum and Khusro Begum. Those women themselves are infatuated with me, and the day you reach to their level, and become one of them, then jealousy would consume you all, and what would happen to you then?

But my entreaties had no effect on them; instead they replied, "We are ready to accept anything. If women are gathered outside, what is the harm in it? No woman can compete with us as regards our status in your presence." Perhaps Nawab Saltanat Begum wanted to move out, simply to learn that whether in this assemblage, I actually preferred the affections of the newer entrants or the senior ones. Holding them by their hands, I escorted them to the gathering outside and let them join the festivities.

In this manner, they descended to the depths of indignity as compared to the exalted status of *mahals*. Shedding all decency and modesty, they joined the multitudes of professional courtesans;

but all this I had done for the sole reason of fulfilling their desire, otherwise it would not have been possible at a later date. When they emerged and joined the others, they tried the usual wiles of coquettishness and coyness, something they used to adopt before joining my establishment. But now, it was no longer possible to flare like a flame as before, because multi-faceted courtesans were now present in the gathering. There was no way that Nawab Sarfaraz could attain their levels. She was determined to be faithless, although she had been well bestowed with all privileges. Things came to such a pass that catfights broke out between the two with Kaiser Begum, Khusro Begum and other *begums* became even more infuriated. On one side, there were just the two of them; consequently it was not a fair or even fight. On the other hand, Saltanat Begum gave evidence of her faithfulness and devotion. But her effort lacked the previous intensity or allurement, and I started to experience the huge distance which had now crept between us.

Eventually, they were left to their own devices, and their acts, good or bad, were generally ignored. I openly informed Sarfaraz that it was no longer possible for me to consort with her, seeing her indiscretions, which had hurt me immensely. That it would be advisable if she could control herself in this regard. She wept aloud on hearing this, because she had no reply. But these incidents shocked me so deeply that my day-to-day activities were severely affected, including my food and sleep. As a result of all this, I dispatched her to her mother, telling myself never to associate with this treacherous person at any cost. But I proved to be helpless due to my heart. She was no longer present in front of my eyes. Finally, I relented and attempted to contact her once again through Qutub-ud-Daula. She responded by conveying that she would not present herself at any cost. Because she had been immensely humiliated. And that now, she would be proceeding on a pilgrimage to *Karbala*.

I grew agitated on getting this response from her, and said, "Qutub-ud-Daula, bring her to me at any cost." On getting this the unfortunate Qutubullah, who had been honoured with the title of

Qutub-ud-Daula Bahadur, again went to her house and persuaded her to come to me. However, I could no longer converse with her as before. Even if on occasion, if I came across her, I would address her obliquely. She retaliated in the same manner, as a form of revenge.

Birth of Mirza Sultan

In those days, the auspicious news regarding the birth of a lovely son from Nawab Mahal Saheba was communicated to me. I thanked the Almighty and celebrated the occasion with the firing of eleven cannons. I was immensely happy with the birth of this son, but destiny willed that the child should die within a year. I was indisposed in those days. The Resident expressed his condolences and assured me of his friendship and support. Ill that I was, this inauspicious news caused further deterioration in my condition. I was unaware of the days and nights passing by.

Weddings of the Princesses

One day I was very dejected and depressed. I felt that I should free myself from the responsibilities of my daughters. Only the Almighty knew what the future held in store for me. After obtaining counsel from my respected mother, I sent out proposals far and wide for the marriage of the princesses. Nawab Mohsin-ud-Daula Bahadur offered to marry his paternal uncle's son, Mirza Ali Qadr with Meher Ara Sugra Begum, daughter of Nawab Izzat Mahal Saheba. The girl was five years old at that time. Mirza Abul Qasim Khan accepted the hand of Sipahr Ara Begum Saheba, for his maternal cousin brother. Similarly, my niece was to be wedded to Mirza Falak Qadr Bahadur.

Shah Manzil[159], situated at the edge of the river, was the venue for all these weddings. I thanked the Almighty after the auspicious event. Musical and dance events were organised once again, after that day, and those present on those events experienced the joy of these for many days.

The Strange Ways of the World

On one occasion, I came to know that Nawab Nishat Mahal, Nanhi Begum Saheba, Nawab Sikandar Mahal Saheba and Umrao Begum were expecting. But these proved to be mere rumours, based on heresy.

During this period, on my orders, Nawab Khurshid Mahal Saheba, Nawab Amir Mahal Saheba and Ajaib Khanum Saheba joined me outside (i.e. out of the *zenana*) in the male quarters. However, due to reasons unknown, even after losing their chastity and modesty, they went back behind the veil. Wonder of wonders! If they had to return to seclusion, why emerge from it all[160]?

It appears that they considered chastity and respectability to be child's play. One day, during a domestic clash, Hazrat Begum and Nawab Saltanat Mahal Saheba sent their male emissaries to the Resident's house to complain. But they were arrested midway. What an irrational and improper behaviour it was, to approach the wrong authority in such matters. It is indeed a strange world.

In those days, Mashuq-e-Khas expressed the desire to consume the ashes of my ring. When I acquiesced, she seemed to forget all about it. This indicated that they were well aware of the ways of the world. During the days of my father, these women had sent recommendations through various men. But I did not like them due to their ugliness.

There were innumerable such incidences concerning the perfidy of the *begums* and the *mahals*. Though I was wealthy, physically attractive, of good character, not lacking in resources and possessing several other fine qualities[161], these people behaved towards me in this manner, although several books had been written in my praise.

In the meantime, I arranged to have several wooden boxes glazed with silver, which would be carried by the royal guards accompanying the king. Any individual could place his petition or grievance in these boxes, which would be presented before me without delay. One day, some envelopes were recovered from these boxes. On examination, they contained unusual and strange accounts of Nawab Umrao Saheb, together with other *mahals* and *begums*. This system of petitioning was discontinued thereafter, because they began to cause me mental agony.

Nawab Sikandar Mahal - A Woman Beyond Comparison

The Lord knows everything. I swear to God that Nawab Sikandar Mahal Saheba was a most unique woman - I had seen very few like her. One day, she said affectionately, "Aye *Jān-é-Alam*, with the grace of Allah, all my desires have been fulfilled. My only desire now is to become your wedded wife."

Bowing my head, I asked her if I was this capable, that I should marry now. Would not the numerous *begums* and courtesans of the palace jeer at me, claiming that I too had lost my senses[2, 162] like late King Nasir-ud-Din Haider? But she was adamant. And not willing to heed to my arguments. Out of sheer desperation, I put the entire matter in the hands of my mother. She acquiesced, saying that there was no harm in it.

Eventually, Sikandar Mahal was made to sit in a room and made to complete the rites of the marriage ceremony. Elaborate arrangements had been made for the wedding. Melodious singers were singing songs. Beautiful dancers were exhibiting their talents. Other than this, the ceremony on the third day of the marriage was also celebrated with extravagance.

Mehboob-e-Alam and Dara Begum

A woman called Mughal was serving in those days, as a maid for the dancing girls of my establishment. Gradually, I developed an extraordinary attraction for her. Like a frenzied madman, I would be seeking to be in her vicinity all the time. She was also in the prime of her youth, seemingly unmoved by either heat or cold. Due to this reason, she also became enamoured with me and joined my harem. I honoured her with the title of Mehboob-e-Alam Nawab

Mughal Saheba[163]. Subsequently, a professional courtesan joined my establishment and was named as Dara Begum. But she was subsequently removed, due to her clash, based on jealousy and malice against Kaiser Begum and Khusro Begum.

Re-organisation of *Parikhana*

Once again, I felt an urgent need to reorganise and refashion *Parikhana*, because the glory of the former *Parikhana* had perished. I summoned former employees and all the beauties to the *Daulat Khana-e-Asafi*[164] and *Panch Mahalla*[165]. Some were allowed to go free, and others were married off. Few desired to proceed on pilgrimage to Karbala, which I permitted. Ten to fifteen of these women, who were among the most beautiful and youthful, I reserved for getting trained in playing sarod and dancing. The detailed account of these women is as follows:

One Pasand-ul-Sultan Alia Begum, former slave girl of Mirza Nasir-ud-Din, who had been sent to *Moti Mahal* by me, after providing her with gifts and honours, was recalled, due to her protestations and lamentations. Three slaves of my honoured (late) father, Niaz-ul Sultan Niaz Begum, Ishrat Pari, Gauhar Pari and slaves of Badshah Begum, *viz*. Gulzar-ul Sultan Abbasi Begum, Musahib Pari and the third, Sahib Pari.

A maid by the name of Farukh Begum, from the days of my grandfather[166] was still around. I gave my respects to Dara Begum Khajista-e-Alam Nawab Humayun Begum Saheba, not because she was a highly esteemed woman, but because it caused jealousy and heartburn among Kaiser Begum, Khusro Begum and others.

Another maid from the times of my grandfather, named Margubil Sultan Azima Begum Saheba died shortly afterwards due to typhoid.

Shah Baksh and Altaf Baksh were memorable from the times of my days as a crown prince. One was honoured as Shah Begum, the other as Altaf Begum and inducted with the *paris*. They underwent training in music and dancing.

Monthly emoluments given to these women ranged from rupees one thousand, one thousand and five hundred, to only five hundred. A woman, who had been an attendant of Badshah Begum[167], was given the title of Argawan Pari.

Shaukat Baksh and Nuzhat Baksh joined my services. Each one was provided with prominent music and dance teachers. The entire day passed in understanding and learning about the finer nuances of song and dance.

Most of the women who had been selected for training had no prior experience or exposure to the performing arts; however, they managed to imbibe it under the guidance provided. Some became adepts, while few could not even pick up A-B-C of music and dance.

Musahib Pari became my pupil. I took so much pain in her musical training that compared to others, she became highly proficient, within a short span of time.

It may be emphasised here that this arrangement at *Parikhana* was not to encourage romance or lust; it was to promote and nurture musical training in those women who had the flair and talent for it.

Indiscretions of the Begums

Despite the fact that both Kaiser Begum and Khusro Begum had reached the status of *begum* simultaneously, my attentions continued to be focussed more on Kaiser Begum. Like a madman, I would follow her around at all times. I would take rest where she slept; I would eat where she ate. On observing this manic fascination of mine for Kaiser, both Khusro Begum and Hazrat Begum would be very envious, but I would not pay heed to them. I would remain immersed in this infatuation from head to toe.

In this manner, the fortunes of Kaiser Begum continued to shine for about a year. I gave her thousands of rupees and the house of Jalal-ud-Din to reside in. All accoutrements for raising her dignity and status were provided to her. My love for her also continued to intensify day by day. I became afflicted with gonorrhoea due to her. As long as the symptoms were mild, I continued to be subservient to her, but her habits resembled those of Mashuq-e-Khas. Her mentality was similar to Khusro Begum. She would laugh and cry at random. Sometimes she would remain aloof, and sometimes she would be determined to be faithless. On observing all this, Hazrat Begum declared one day that she would no longer stay in my establishment. I tried to reason with her, but she ordered her carriage and departed for her home. Other than being sorrowful and full of regret, there was nothing I could do.

I instructed Nishat-ud-Daula, the *daroga* in-charge of singers and dancers, to keep surveillance on Hazrat Begum from a distance. He abided by my orders. My attachment for Hazrat Begum decreased after her departure, and it proved to be a problem for her mother also, who had to keep an eye on her, as a mark of respect and regard for me. After a gap of a few months, I called her back to *Parikhana*, through Dayanat-ud-Daula Bahadur.

Because I was enamoured with Hazrat Begum, I did not feel like relinquishing her custody, although there were countless women available like her. For some time, she was included among the group of singers. However, her feelings were now ambivalent towards me and I also did not have the same ardour for her. On those days, I had to journey to Kanpur to met the Lord[168]. While the senior members of my establishment looked after my day-to-day needs, none of the recent *begums* could prove their worth. This was another reason for my change of feelings towards them.

Another reason was that Kaiser Begum had invited her mother to stay with her, despite the fact that she had all comforts provided to her in *Kaiserbagh*. I allowed this, to keep her happy, but she could not appreciate this gesture of mine. Khusro Begum also indulged in similar indiscretions.

One day, I was taking a ride around *Hazrat Bagh* in my buggy, with Mehboob-e-Alam and Hazrat Begum; the latter was in my arms and I was whispering sweet nothings to her. This could not be tolerated by Mehboob-e-Alam and swooning, she fell down from the carriage. By God's grace, her bones remained intact, instead of being broken.

The Effort of Years Devastated in a Moment

Some days had gone by and I was engrossed in checking out the fidelity of different women through various means, with particular reference to the faithfulness of Kaiser Begum and Khusro Begum. Even though I was already aware of the activities of Hazrat Begum, I acted ignorant. One day, I jokingly said that if all of you went back to your homes, I would be relieved from a headache. On hearing this, Hazrat Begum and a few others immediately expressed their intention to leave. Although Umrao Begum did not want to go, because she was expecting at that time. I immediately arranged for carriages, ignoring the protestations of my courtiers. Mehboob-e-Alam was among those who wanted to leave - the one who had earlier been willing to commit suicide by getting crushed under the wheels of my buggy. While leaving, she stated that she would be deputing her servants and palanquin bearers to take stock of my condition in future.

In brief, some *begums* left for their homes, accompanied by Mutim-ud-Daula Bahadur and Musahib-ud-Daula Bahadur, on my assurance that I would not henceforth trouble them in any manner.

No One Enquired After Homecoming

I had always understood that Kaiser Begum was infatuated with me, because she had adopted certain ways, redolent of those times. But it was all a deception. These women, after returning to their homes never enquired about my well-being. However, seeing that benefit could be extracted from the situation, one morning, Hazrat Begum, accompanied by Gulzar Begum and Badshah Begum reached the home of Razi-ud-Daula, and wept aloud, embracing me and declaring that although I was free to behead them, they would never ever leave me. I returned their embrace, but I was aware of the fact that these women had done the same things before also. Therefore, their weeping did not have any significant effect on me.

I was no longer attached to Kaiser Begum as before. The same evening, she approached me, but I did not respond much. I had been proven wrong in my belief that this very Kaiser Begum, who shared her meals with me every day, could ever leave me and return to her own home, which she had done.

Moat-mud-Daula had earlier informed me that the grandmother of Khusro Begum had conveyed to him about the imminent return of Khusro Begum to her own home. The prevailing situation indicated Khusro Begum had apprised her through some person, and hence the grandmother had awaited her at *Dar-e-Daulat* for some time. When Khusro Begum departed in her carriage, I strew coins at the beggars and seekers of alms lining the path. I also arranged for a feast in honour of Hazrat Ali and other celebrations. Khusro Begum herself appeared like a flower in full bloom. In her ecstasy and happiness, she would embrace people around her. Sometimes she would laugh aloud in gay abandon.

I came to know that Mehboob-e-Alam was not happy after returning to her home. There was similar news of Imtiaz Begum also.

I was particularly offended that among those seven to eight *begums*, not one held my hand and stated that she would not leave me. This was the reason that from that day onwards, I would stay clear of all *begums*, and never pine for anyone's affections. I was now so repelled by the female sex, that had any woman died, I would have felt that she had entered her grave as part of some new conspiracy. I would not rest in peace till *Chehlum*[169] had been observed for her.

Eventually, the *begums* did re-enter my household, but against convention - those who had to join later appeared earlier.

Hazrat Begum, Gulzar Begum and Badshah Begum arrived first, although Kaiser Begum, Khusro Begum, Imtiaz Begum and Mehboob-e-Alam should have come earlier. Hazrat Begum cunningly came before Kaiser Begum and Khusro Begum. I accommodated Kaiser Begum near me to irk the others, remaining indifferent towards the others. I did not embrace any of them, and remained silent. How would the others respond, on hearing that Hazrat Begum, Badshah Begum and Gulzar Begum had declared that they did not want to leave? After some time, I came to know that Khusro Begum wanted to leave a second time. Similarly, Mehboob-e-Alam also observed that Gulzar Begum, who had actually initiated the return, now shared similar views with Khusro Begum and Mehboob-e-Alam. Although Hazrat Begum remained steadfast in her declaration.

I had heard the conversation among the three with my own ears, which pained me immensely and I mentally noted, "O you good-for-nothing, unworthy women, you yourself are responsible for your own predicament." Utterly fed up with their perfidy and betrayal, I pressed my hands to my breast and stated, "All right. Do whatever you feel like." But I realised that the final test rested with me, and to leave them to their fate would not be wise.

Although I gave them permission, I secretly instructed my courtiers to advise the women thus, "Whether you enter the household of a beggar or a soldier, your movements would still be restricted, and here you were in the house of a king."

In this manner, when they realised that there was no option, other than asking for mercy and forgiveness, they fell at my feet and asked to be pardoned. Because I was myself interested in maintaining a relationship with them once again, I agreed and granted them pardon. I was interested in elevating the status of Kaiser Begum as compared to Mashuq-e-Khas, and others, so she might become unmatched and supreme in due course of time. Accordingly, I allowed her to attend social occasions and celebrations, while constraints remained for the others.

I desired that Kaiser Begum should desist from attending social functions on her own accord, but she did not pay heed to this. She maintained her social contacts with other *mahals* and *begums*, especially Nawab Sarfaraz Mahal. In those days, Nawab Sarfaraz Mahal was among the outer circle of *begums*; because she was an adept as far as infidelity was concerned. In fact, Nawab Sarfaraz Mahal Saheba, who was an excessively envious woman, was desirous that the other women should also follow her footsteps. Hence, she was exceedingly hospitable towards Kaiser Begum.

Kaiser Begum started taking an interest in the company of Sarfaraz Begum, which was not acceptable to me.. During the wedding of the princesses, she had accompanied the *mahals* and *begums* who had proceeded to *Shah Manzil*[159]. But it was a humiliating experience for her. I was also pained at this. Whenever I would go to a *Khas Mahal*, she would try to accompany me. I would try to persuade her and explain to her to desist, but she would not heed. I would tell her that my heart was no longer with the *Khas Mahals,* and I met them only for the sake of family obligations and convention. That it was not proper for her to accompany me, and also be humiliated. This was due to the fact that I would be hospitable[170] during my visit to any *mahal*. At that moment, I would not spare any thought for her. And if this was acceptable to her, then she could accompany me.

She would accept this condition, but my heart sickened due to all this.

Another woman, who was given the title of Zohra Begum, entered my household in those days. Also, I swore to myself that henceforth, I would no longer indulge in love play with any woman.

I Became Helpless in This Manner Also

In those days, I had become afflicted with gonorrhoea due to my relations with Kaiser Begum. My condition worsened steadily. There was a feeling of having being set on fire. Sadly, the women also remained upset about my condition. I asked myself, that when I had been healthy and devoid of any affliction, then the women had no sympathisers, so from where had the sympathisers appeared now? Coincidentally, one day, after touching my body, Mehboob-e-Alam Nawab Mughal Saheba cleaned her hands with flour, before my very eyes. On observing this, I wept. Not only this, but she approached me and stated, "May the Lord cure you. This is a contagious disease. It is dangerous to touch a patient having this disease. Due to this reason, I cleaned my hands thus." On hearing this - I remained silent, but secretly wept in seclusion. From that day onwards, I made the *Shahanshah Manzil* off bounds, not allowing anybody to come close to me.

The other *begums* wanted to present themselves. But such was the effect of Mehboob-e-Alam's conduct that I did not allow anyone to approach me. I did not mention this to anybody. Because I had been truly afflicted by a fatal disease. Instead of subsiding, the disease seemed to progress day-by-day. I spent sleepless nights in its agony. Several treatments were tried, many medicines consumed, yet there was no relief.

This occurred in 1265 *Hijri*[171] . The eruptions and sores had subsided and dried; abstinence was being observed. But there was no relief from the agony and discomfort. I observed the *Chehlum* of Hazrat Imam Hussain and out of sheer desperation, consumed chopped *har*[172]. As a result of which, my palpitations did decrease somewhat. But I tore my clothes apart. The next day, I also swooned. My eyes remained closed. My relatives and the kinder hearted *begums* started lamenting. I remained prostrate the whole night, despite their ministrations. I was not aware of anything around me.

Two months have elapsed since that fateful day. Sores erupt and subside by themselves. I am bound by this illness. I am unaware of the world. When I briefly come to my senses, I engage myself in reciting poetry, but within a short span of time, the same symptoms reappear. I start trembling like a leaf in the wind. I am even unable to recite *namaz*[100], such is my helplessness. May the Lord have mercy on me.

Verily I have seen with my own eyes that in those tragic times, the *begums* would put on new clothes, adorn themselves and move hither and thither, enjoying the pleasures of song and dance. When I observed their inconsiderate, insensitive and thoughtless behaviour, I shifted to the house of Razi-ud-Daula, so I would not come face to face with these fake and unfaithful women. Kaiser Begum was also stricken with the same disease during the same period. Her body became covered with sores. Actually, I had contracted this affliction from her only. However, her health improved within two to three months, but my condition remained the same. Then I came to know that Imtiaz Begum had contracted the same disease. She continues to ail, during the time of writing these lines. Sometimes, she would be in her senses, and at other times, she would remain unconscious.

Hazrat Begum and Mehboob-e-Alam continued their indiscretions during this tragic period. Hazrat Begum had a show-down with me and left for her house. She also consumed a *tola*[145] of opium. This was another shock that I had to bear. Out of desperation, I went to her house, with the aid of others and managed to get her to vomit. The Lord showered his mercy on me.

Another incident of those days of sickness. Once, leaving me in the care of *hakims*[173], Mehboob-e-Alam and Khusro Begum mounted a carriage and went for a pleasure jaunt, without informing me. There had been a time when I was hale and hearty, and yet, had never thought of proceeding on a joyride without them. And now, here I was, helpless because of my ailment.

When I objected to this behaviour, Mehboob-e-Alam expressed regret and branded her left thigh with my royal seal. Although I observed this with my own eyes, I remained unmoved.

All the while, Hazrat Begum and Mehboob-e-Alam continued their perfidious activities. Occasionally, they would bicker, and then make up. One day they scorned me in the presence of Nawab Khas Mahal Saheba. But I remained silent. If they remained with me for three days, then they would be with others for the next three days. May Allah save us and protect us from such treacherous women. I expressed my displeasure and weariness with all musical instruments, as a result of which, henceforth, no melody reached my ears. This apathy of mine resulted in the destruction of the entire *Parikhana.*

Demise of Mirza Falak Qadr

The news of Mirza Falak Qadr Bahadur's tragic demise reached me during my days of illness. That child who was the *Wali Ahad* (crown prince, heir designate), had been stricken by TB. He bid farewell from this world due to this disease.

My back was literally broken due to my own illness. Tragedy came upon me like a cloudburst. But what could be done, except to keep patience and express gratitude.

Few Strange Incidents

Mehboob-e-Alam Nawab Mughal Saheba and Sultan Hazrat Mahal Saheba were residing with me in the house of Razi-ud-Daula, without any valid reason. The access of other *begums* was totally prohibited. One day, the other *begums*, through mutual consent, put a wooden ladder which reached till the terrace, and all of them climbed inside, destroying locks and doors in the process. When I observed that Hazrat Mahal Saheba was also liable to move away from me, I decided that flattery was a way out, and hence shunned those women who had forcibly entered the premises, *viz*. Mushqul Sultan Khusro Begum Saheba, Ashiqul Sultan Mumtaz Alam Nawab Kaiser Begum Saheba, and Mehboob-ul Sultan Badshah Begum Saheba. I even avoided looking at them.

Despite my medical condition, Ashiqul Sultan Mumtaz Alam Nawab Kaiser Begum Saheba started pleading to grant them permission to indulge in song and dance. Similarly, Mashuq-e-

Khas Malk-e-Mahe Alam Nawab Sultanat Mahal Saheba expressed her desire to listen to songs. When I had been healthy, there had been no restriction on any woman for this sort of entertainment, but due to my health, I had to refuse permission. But these accursed women carried on nevertheless with their song and dance routines.

This incident irked Wazir-ul-Mulk Nawab Ali Naqi Khan - that despite the painful condition of the ruler, some people were engaged in such frivolous activities. He issued stern orders that henceforth no singer or musician would be allowed in the presence of His Majesty, and likewise, neither were the *begums* and *mahals* were allowed in to present themselves. Strict implementation of this created a new set of problems. Requests for allowing song and dance reached me, which I did not entertain at all. There was an unwritten law that if a woman enters a Hindu household, she has to adopt Hinduism, and if she enters a Muslim household, she has to adopt the Muslim faith. Then why did these women want to indulge in the very activities which I had prohibited and which had affected my health adversely. It was obvious that these women had a treacherous nature and wanted to be occupied with such activities, even if I was indisposed.

In fact, Kaiser Begum stated, "I am not willing to stay with you. Either you allow me to be involved in music and song, or else, let me proceed to my own home." In my helpless condition, I granted her permission to leave, but Lord knows why, she did not proceed.

Because these five women had barged into the house where I was residing (known as Razi-ud-Daula's house) with this intention, I ignored them totally. They exclaimed, "Show us some hospitality; we have come to you for this very reason." On the other hand, Hazrat Begum Saheba wanted to remain aloof and enjoy exclusive rights. This resulted in further discord as the rivalry escalated rapidly. All the *begums* mentioned above decided to reside with me, and thus this domestic tumult continued for five days. During this period, Mehboob-e-Alam came near me, glowering, "Your sickness is not my concern." I raised my eyes to the heavens and remained silent. One day I observed that despite being forbidden by me, Mehboob-e-Alam was playing a game of cards. This also irked me considerably.

When I grew weary of all this, I had all the women forcibly removed from the premises and sent to the palace. Although Hazrat Mahal continued to reside with me in Razi-ud-Daula's house. When the others were evicted in this manner, their demeanour resembled that of a black, hissing serpent. Meanwhile, Hazrat Mahal cooed, "If you stop meeting me, God promise, I will commit suicide." Eventually, it was mutually accepted by both of us that I would do what I wished to do, and likewise, she would be free to do what she desired to do.

One day, on the occasion of *Eid-ul-Zuha* (*Bakra Eid*)[61], I went to *Badshah Manzil*[175] to pay respects to my mother. There was a great gathering there, with the *begums* and *mahals*. At night, the *begums* and their courtiers gathered (numbering to about three to four thousand in number) together, with the sole intention of publicly humiliating Hazrat Begum. Accordingly, all entries and exits of the premises were sealed off and all movements, to and fro, were restricted. When Hazrat Begum came to know of all this, she concealed a dagger in the folds of her garments, with the intention of committing suicide. After midnight, I mounted my palanquin, and just as the bearers were about to lift the palanquin, Hazrat Begum pleaded, "O *Jān-é-Alam*! I shall also accompany you." Because I was unaware of the circumstances, I replied, "*Bismillah*! Please come[176]." Hazrat Begum climbed inside and sat on my right side.

The palanquin bearers had barely lifted the palanquin, when Mushqul Sultan and Mehboob-e-Alam attempted to encircle her with a whip with the intention of dragging her out. Few other women also joined the fray, surrounding the palanquin, as Mehboob-e-Alam tried to wrap the whip around Hazrat Begum's neck and make her tumble out of the palanquin. At that very moment, Hazrat Begum drew her dagger, with an intention to stab herself. But I slipped my hand between her chest and the dagger. It was a terrible moment, impossible to describe in words.

Eventually, after a lot of discussion and negotiations, and intervention by my esteemed mother, it was decided that I would devote seven hours daily to Hazrat Begum Saheba, and one hour with the others. Accordingly, from that moment onwards, to the present day, I have maintained this practice. An attendant deputed by my respected mother arrives every day, and I accompany him to the company of the other *begums*, with whom I spend an hour, and then return.

But even this arrangement is not acceptable to Hazrat Begum Saheba, and my heart is also not into this practice of meeting these unfaithful women; time alone will tell how things will develop in the future[177]. In those days, I came to know that Umrao Begum Saheba had had an *Imambara*[178] constructed surreptitiously, and due to some internal conflict, I was not aware of the fact. Later, I even chastised her on this issue.

Tragedy of Jahanara Begum

During 20 *Zu al-Hijjah* 1265 [179], a fresh tragedy was in my fate. God's gift and darling daughter of Fiza Habshin[87], Jahanara Begum departed from this world at the age of three years. My eyes clouded with grief and I was rent asunder with the arrows of bereavement. May God grant her a place under his mercy and protection.

Kaiwan Qadr Bahadur as *Wali Ahad*

Mirza Falak Qadr, *Wali Ahad*, had departed from this world at the tender age of eight years. The position of *Wali Ahad* had thus become vacant. After a lot of thought, his younger brother, Mirza Kaiwan Qadr Bahadur was honoured as the new *Wali Ahad*. Mirza Faridoon Qadr Bahadur, the son of Mallika Taj un-Nisa was given the post of *Jarnail*[30]. The auspicious day of conferring these honours was *Shaban* 15th, of the Islamic calendar, an auspicious day[174]. May the Lord be merciful.

Nawab Sikandar Mahal Departs

After some days had passed, another harrowing and heart-breaking news left me numb - the demise of faithful Nawab Sikandar Mahal. She had been suffering from heart ailment. When this news reached my ears, I wept tears of blood. Words were insufficient to describe my grief for this devoted friend.

Faithful and Unfaithful Lovers

Mashuq-e-Khas, Mallika-e-Alan, Nawab Saltanat Mahal Saheba, Mehboob-e-Khas Jane Jahan Ashiqnuma Nawab Dildar Mahal Saheba, Habib-ul-Sultan, Muqarram-ul-Zamani Nawab Sikandar Mahal Saheba, Khurshid-ul Saheba, Nishat Mahal, Nawab Nanhi Begum Saheba, all these were steadfast, trustworthy women. All others remaining were deceitful. The Lord knows better.

From among the eight new *begums*, none could be considered as trustworthy. I hope that whomsoever will read this treatise on deceit, shall stay away from the enchantment of women. And neither shall he waste time on them, because the result of this is no secret. Such women would not hesitate to deceive even a divine messenger such as Hazrat Yusuf. Hence it is best to stay away (from such women).

If they were not in awe of a king such as I, who was incomparable in looks and ability, in whose praise, so many books had been written, then what would their conduct be with regard to others.

5

Annotations

1. *Maulvi:* Islamic scholar; a learned and religious man; interpreter of Islamic law.
2. Nasir-ud-Din Haider, the second king of Awadh ruled from October 19, 1827 to July 7, 1837. History has tarnished him as a quirky, British-centric ruler, who was apparently under the influence of a European barber, George Derusett. But it is also true that he was responsible for creating / building a number of institutions in Lucknow, including an observatory (*Taaron Wali Kothi*), hospitals and library (*Gulistan-e-Iram*).
3. Munna Jaan: Successor apparent to Nasir-ud-Din Haider, but repudiated by him later. His candidature was vociferously supported by Badshah Begum, dowager queen of Ghazi-ud-Din Haider, which led to a conflict with the British. Both Munna Jaan and Badshah Begum were deported to Chunar fort in exile.
4. *Dogana*: Indicating an intimate friendship between two people.
5. *Ganjfa*: *Ganjifa, Ganjapa* or *Gānjaphā*, is a card game and type of playing cards mostly associated with then Persia (Iran) and India. After *Ganjifa* cards fell out of use in Iran before the twentieth century, India became the last country to produce them. The form prevalent in Odisha is called Ganjapa.
6. *Hammam:* Turkish bath.

7. *Laila Majnu*: Old Arabic love story about Qais (a common man) and Layla (a princess), often called Romeo and Juliet of the East.
8. *Chakladar:* Administrative division under a province; person heading the *chakla*.
9. *Muh boli:* No literal translation or explanation of the term exists. Denotes a relation, merely by word-of-mouth and mutual acceptance, but devoid of blood ties. For example, a *muh boli beti* will indicate a girl, who has been accepted in a family as a daughter (not necessarily with legal rights), although there is no blood relation between her and her (foster) parents.
10. Nawab Sayyid Ali Khan Bahadur's wife, Barati Khanum was supposedly a daughter of Claude Martin. Their daughter, Mallika Muqqadara-i-Azma Nawab Alam Ara Begum (=queen), titled as Badshah Mahal Saheba and first wife of Wajid Ali Shah remained as *Khas Mahal* or senior-most consort of Wajid Ali Shah. Also known as Nawab Azam Bahu Saheba, she was a poetess in her own right, writing under the *nom de plume* of 'Alam.'
11. *Manje ki rasam*: This ceremony is held four days before the actual wedding day in a Muslim marriage. There is a dress code for the groom as well as the guests (predominantly yellow – orange). The bride-to-be is also dressed in yellow clothes and turmeric paste is applied on her body. After this, the bride is not supposed to step out of her house.
12. *15 Shaban, 1253 Hijri*, converted to the Gregorian equivalent works out to be November 14, 1837.
13. Nasir-ud-Daula Nawab Mirza Asghar Ali Bahadur was the eldest son of Mohammad Ali Shah, the third king of Awadh, who ruled during 1837 – 42. Being the third son of Sa'adat Ali Khan, who was Nawab of Awadh during 1798 – 1814, Mohammad Ali Shah had not in the direct line of succession of Awadh's rulers. Sa'adat Ali Khan had been succeeded by

Ghazi-ud-Din Haider (1814 – 17), followed by Nasir-ud-Din Haider (1827 – 37). After Nasir-ud-Din Haider's untimely demise, and problems in his succession, the British brought in Mohammad Ali Shah to rule over Awadh. Mohammad Ali Shah, already advanced in his years, briefly ruled Awadh for 5 years. However, his rule was a capable one. He would be succeeded by Amjad Ali Shah (1842 – 47) and finally the dynasty would culminate with Wajid Ali Shah (1847- 56), the last king of Awadh.

14. *Takht Nashini*: Enthronement or accession to the throne; ceremonial installation of a ruler / king. Equivalent to *taj poshi* or coronation. Wajid Ali Shah refers to his late father by the epithet, *Jannat Makān*, or one who has an abode in the heavens = beatified.
15. By the time Wajid Ali Shah wrote this narrative, Mohammad Ali Shah, his grandfather, was already dead. Hence, Wajid Ali has respectfully referred to him as *Firdaus Manzil* or one who has ascended to paradise (*firdaus*).
16. Wajid Ali Shah's father, "Hazrat" Amjad Ali Shah was the fifth son of Mohammad Ali Shah, from his second wife, Khetu Begum or Mariam Makani. Although not in the direct line of succession, he had been appointed as heir apparent (*Wali Ahad*) on October 15, 1837, with the titles of *Suraiya Jah* and *Wali Ahad Mirza Bahadur*.
17. Despite his auspicious birth and accompanying festivities, he was not to be heir apparent to the Awadh throne as he was physically challenged (deaf and dumb). This ill-fated line continued, with Shahzada Falak Qadr, Mirza Mohammad Javed Ali Khan, Hashim Saheba, although *Wali Ahad* (crown prince) died from small pox in 1849.
18. This seems to have been the turning point in Wajid Ali's life: (a) it turned him from an amorous youthful lover to a poet of standing and (b) it started a long-drawn out confrontation with his chief queen, *Khas Mahal* Alam Ara Begum, which was to

last all throughout his life. Alam Ara Begum outlived her husband – she died on March 13, 1894, and was buried in the family mausoleum in *Metia Burz*, Calcutta.

19. Shahzada Kaiwan Qadr, Mirza Mohammad Hamid Ali, was the third son of Alam Ara Begum, born in 1838. Although he became *Wali Ahad* after the untimely death of his elder brother (see above), the ill-fated line continued, because he could never succeed Wajid Ali Shah as king - the latter was deposed by the British in 1856. Mirza Hamid Ali accompanied his grandmother, Mallika Kishwar, to London for pleading Awadh's case before Queen Victoria in London. The efforts came to naught, and Mallika Kishwar died on their return journey. In the meantime, Birjis Qadr had been declared as Wajid Ali Shah's successor by a section of freedom fighters camping at Lucknow, so effectively, Hamid Ali lost his inheritance also. He died in 1874 and was buried in the family mausoleum at *Metia Burz*.

20. *Paan*: *Pān*, a preparation composed of shards of areca nut, slaked lime and catechu, sometimes with flavoured tobacco, wrapped with a fresh green betel leaf, thereby creating a triangular bundle. Always prepared by hand, *paan* is chewed for its stimulant and psychoactive effects. It is hugely popular in SE Asian countries, although the adverse effects of this combination are well documented.

21. Trellis: A door having an open framework or lattice, of interwoven or intersecting pieces of wood, bamboo or metal. Handy for climbing plants and general ventilation.

22. *Sitar*: Stringed instrument mainly used in Hindustani music. Actually a modification of the *Veena*, and named after the *Setar*, a three-stringed Persian instrument. It is not clear whether Wajid Ali refers to the *sitar* or the *setar* here.

23. *Zakira* and *majlis*: Imam Husain was one of the two grandsons of the Prophet Mohammad, being the younger of the two sons of Hazrat Fatima, the daughter of the Holy Prophet. Since the

Holy Prophet had no surviving sons of his own, out of affection, he referred to Hasan and Hussain as his "sons." In 680 AD, Hussain Ali and his family members were martyred in the plains of Karbala, Iraq, while fighting Yazid, the self-styled sixth Caliph of Islam. *Majlis* denotes a congregation of the devout. A *zakira* is a female who recites elegies *(marsiyas)* related to Muharram during a *majlis*. The *Ishqnama* states that they were Mir Insha's daughters (*dukhtar*). In the *Parikhana* (Tehsin Sarwari, 1965) the author says they were his granddaughters (*nawāsîān*).

24. *Mahal:* A spouse, *nikah* or *mut'ah*, who had given birth to a son.
25. *Shirin Farhad*: A famous Persian tragic love story, about Sasanian king Khosrow II and Armenian princess Shirin.
26. *Marsiya*: Dirge, elegy, epicedium, especially as a genre of poetry commemorating Imam Hussain's martyrdom at Karbala (see above).
27. *Dariya mein rehkar magarmach se bair*: Literally translates to "living in a river and having the crocodile as an enemy." Hindustani equivalent of "You cannot live in Rome and fight with the Pope." Denotes the futility of fighting with someone who is more powerful, and whom, one is dependent upon.
28. *Char din ki chandni, fir andheri raat*: Literally translates to, "Four days of moonlight followed by dark nights." Loose Hindustani equivalent of "A nine days' wonder." Denotes that pleasurable days are transient, and are invariably followed by trouble.
29. Although not explicitly stated in the narrative, three women appear to have been present in the scene during the year 1842: Nanhi Begum, Umda Begum and Afshar un-Nisan Begum.
30. *Jarnail* Mirza Sikandar Hashmat Bahadur: It was a tradition in those days that the younger brother of the ruling king (or

heir apparent) would lead the imperial forces as General or *Jarnail.*

31. *Mujra:* Singing and dancing by courtesans (see below).
32. *Tawa'if:* Courtesan or nautch girl. *Tawa'ifs* were an integral part of Nawabi culture of Lucknow. Equally comfortable in the royal court, *kothas* and residences of the wealthy, the courtesans of Lucknow, from diverse ethnic and caste backgrounds, having musical skills and artistic abilities also wielded political influence, due to their Nawabi connections. Courtesans could not only recite the *marsiya* and *soz* in a *majlis*, they were highly proficient in the performing arts as well. Their social skills were frequently made use of by wealthy patrons for instruction in etiquette, genteelness and refined language. The contribution of Lucknow's courtesans in the development of musical *thumris*, *ghazals*, and the dance choreography of the classical *kathak* is well established. Many courtesans were quite wealthy in their own right, and consorting with them did not have the social stigma, that came to be associated later on. In fact, it was a social symbol in those days. The *tawa'if* culture reached its zenith during the rule of Awadh's last king, Wajid Ali Shah, who had a dedicated *Parikhana* for them, and staged *Indrasabhas* in his court at *Kaiserbagh*, Lucknow. After the annexation of Awadh in 1856, and the declining fortunes of the Awadh nobility, the patronage of the courtesans also came to an end.
33. *Daroga*: Superintendent (of police / guards); on guard duty.
34. *Wazir*: (Prime) Minister.
35. *Sayyid*: Sayyad: An honorific title denoting people accepted as descendants of the Prophet Mohammad and his cousin and son-in-law Ali through his grandsons, Hasan Ali and Hussain Ali. Female Sayyids are given the titles Sayyida, Syeda, Alawiyah or Sharifa.
36. *Thumri*: A vocal genre or style of Indian music, romantic or devotional in nature, the lyrics usually in north Indian dialects

of Hindi called *Awadhi* and *Braj Bhasha*. *Thumri* is characterised by its sensuality and flexibility.

37. *Huzoor:* Addressing a person of high rank, or a title; respect for such a person.

38. From the narrative, Mir Mohammad Mehdi appears to have played a significant role in bringing Wajid Ali's object of desire to him. But Wajid Ali honours Amin-ud-Daula with robes and titles for his unwavering loyalty and services provided. This anomaly is not explained subsequently in the text.

39. *Kos:* During the Mughal period, a distance of one *kos* was roughly equal to 3 kms.

40. Hazrat Ali: Cousin, son-in-law, companion and successor of Prophet Mohammad, as per Shi'a theology.

41. Females and transgenders were often appointed as guards in harems, due to obvious reasons.

42. *Khwajasara:* Transgender; often holding high position in the Nawabi court.

43. *Huma* bird in Iranian mythology is equivalent to the mythical Phoenix. *Huma* is considered to be compassionate, and a 'bird of good fortune' since its shadow (or appearance) is said to be auspicious. In the present allegory, Wajid Ali compares himself to this powerful bird and the *huzur-e-wali* women as low born, comparable to crows. Evidently he cannot be benefited, by loving such lowly women and neither can he be harmed.

44. *Sitar:* See above.

45. Mohammad Ali Shah, third king of Awadh.

46. *Shayari*: Composing and recitation of couplets.

47. Baiju, Gopal and Tansen: Prominent court musicians during Mughal rule.

48. *Ustad*: Maestro; instructor.

49. *Pari:* Fairy or celestial nymph. Before this, the women had been given loftier titles by Wajid Ali Shah and even included

in the harem as *mahals* or wives. The status of a *pari* was obviously much lower, suited to her role as a glorified entertainer and nothing else. Later, the British would deprecatingly refer to these *paris* as nautch (singing as dancing) girls. Did Wajid Ali's distressing experience with the *huzur-e-walia* made him petulant and disappointed with the female sex as a whole?

50. *Izzat Pari and Mahrukh Pari*, although described in different paragraphs, turn out to be mother and daughter. The irony is not lost on the reader, as Wajid Ali Shah candidly describes the conduct of mother and daughter, together with the dubious role of a *daroga* or guard in the entire unsavoury episode. That the mother could happily sell off her daughter for a sum of rupees five hundred, albeit to the harem of a royal prince, speaks volumes of the social mores prevalent at that time.
51. *Domni*: The *dom* caste has ancient origins; few writers have theorised that they are a branch of gypsies, who may have migrated to North India. *Doms* are considered to be low in the caste hierarchy, engaged in marginal agriculture, weaving, sweeping and scavenging. They are primarily engaged in the disposal of animal carcasses and also cremation of dead bodies. Due to extreme poverty and social *ostracisation*, their women (*domni*) may not above petty prostituting to make ends meet.
52. Dancing girls, nautch girls, courtesans, prostitutes and women of similar professions did not carry the stigma that they do in present times (see above). It was a status symbol to be associated with such women. Many such ladies were also immensely rich, as well as musically talented.
53. *Dargah:* Tomb of Muslim saint, often used for prayers and for asking favours / boons.
54. This unsavoury incident in an open gathering does not bring any glory to Wajid Ali Shah. In history, there are several instances of Mirza Sikandar Hashmat displaying greater maturity and equanimity, while his elder brother continued with his profligate ways. But the honesty of Wajid Ali Shah

has to be noted, as he candidly describes this incident, without any regret or sense of remorse.

55. *Itr:* Perfume; essence.

56. *Parikhana* or *Pari Khana:* House or Abode of Fairies. The first was obviously a modest house, which was dedicated to training singing and dancing girls of Wajid Ali Shah's court. No record of the name or location of this house or building is known. It can be conjectured that it might have been present in the *Chattar Manzil* seraglio, because *Kaiserbagh* did not exist then. The *Parikhana* proper would be created by Wajid Ali Shah inside the *Kaiserbagh* in later years, when he became the king of Awadh.

57. *Lā hawla wa lā quwwat*: The full phrase, *Lā hawla wa lā quwwata illā bi Allāh*, is mentioned numerous times in the *hadith* as being highly regarded and highly recommended by the Prophet Mohammad. The phrase is part of the daily prayers for many Muslims, and is commonly used in ceremony and *zikr*. Loosely translated, it means, *there is neither change (transformation) nor power (strength) except through Allāh.*

58. *Tabla:* A percussion instrument, composed of two small hand drums, commonly used in the Indian sub-continent, both for solo performances as well as for accompaniment.

59. *Bahar-e-Mehfil:* Literally translates to springtime of a cultural gathering. But denotes a person who is the life and soul of a musical soiree.

60. This unpleasant episode indicates another aspect of the *Parikhana* – that women who did not accept Wajid Ali's overtures could be coerced into joining his establishment. This was the first such incident in Wajid Ali's own words and gives a totally new dimension to the vision of *Parikhana* hitherto given – that of a happy place, full of consenting women, singing and dancing, and of course, madly in love with the prince / king.

61. *Eid:* There are two official festivals in Islam: *Eid-ul-Fitr*, which marks the end of the month long dawn-to-sunset fasting of *Ramzan*, and *Eid-ul-Zuha*, which honours the willingness of Ibrahim (Abraham) to sacrifice his son Ismael as an act of obedience to God's command.
62. *Shab-e-Barat:* Observed on the 15th night (the night between the 14th and 15th) of the month of Sha'ban, the eighth month of the Islamic calendar. In most regions, it is a night when one's deceased ancestors are commemorated. *Shab-e-Barat* is a major event in the Islamic calendar, when Muslims collectively worship and ask for forgiveness for their wrong-doings.
63. A third aspect of *Parikhana* – trafficking in women. However, society and royalty of those times had a different set of rules, no longer applicable today. We had earlier seen money exchanging hands in the case of Waziran, who was freed from the clutches of her hawk-like mother, Bi Jaan, after payment of rupees two thousand and clothes to the latter. But this time, a mother happily peddles off her daughter (albeit a courtesan) after signing consent papers. Whatever might have been the social mores of those times, economic considerations ruled the roost (as they still do). Dancing exclusively for a royal audience, with free boarding and lodging was obviously preferable to dancing for the public, leading to financial uncertainty and lack of social status.
64. *Sharia*: Islamic law.
65. *Rajab*: The seventh month of the Islamic calendar. *Nauchandi* denotes the new moon.
66. The veil-less beauties, in full regalia, had apparently caused a ruckus among the bystanders and public, which irked the king, Amjad Ali Shah. Wajid Ali Shah had realised earlier that at the first opportunity, a courtesan, however cloistered, would revert back to her original profession by exposing her face and dilly-dallying with strangers. The public visit to the *dargah*

would be an acid test for them – a test which the *paris* unfortunately failed.

67. Nawab Nishat Mahal was previously Nanhi Begum, whose exploits we have read earlier, including an attempt to commit suicide from the *Chattar Manzil* palace. *Suleiman Pari* was apparently the daughter of Ghulam Raza, but this has not been mentioned explicitly in the text.

68. A dichotomy here. A female attendant, not a *pari*, became pregnant – she was put behind *purdah* or veil, but not given the honour of being a *mahal*, a title loosely used for wives or concubines who gave birth to Wajid Ali's offspring. A caste system obviously existed within the confines of the household, a system wholly defined by Wajid Ali himself.

69. The first brief (not so flattering) reference to a woman who would later get the title of *Iftikhar un-Nisan*, and become famous as Begum Hazrat Mahal.

70. *Gulzar Manzil*: This building is untraceable now.

71. Wajid Ali Shah's self description is undoubtedly lyrical and full of hyperbole. Unfortunately, on second thought, it is both tragic and comic. Tragic - because of his personal world distancing itself from that of a crown prince - destined to rule over a prosperous kingdom. Instead of acquiring skills in politics, governance and administration, he was slowly getting immersed in the bottomless pit of sensuousness. Comic - because it would be difficult for history to justify his unhealthy interest in women, particularly women from the lower strata of society, by referring to his concurrent expertise in song / dance. The two did not have any logical connection.

72. Ghulam Raza would consolidate his position tremendously in the court of Wajid Ali Shah, particularly when the latter became king. He came to the notice of the British also, as subsequent events would indicate.

73. *Musahibané Khurd:* Literally means junior companions or courtiers.

74. Shahzada Faridun Qadr, Mirza Mohammad Hizabir Ali Bahadur was born to Mashuq Mahal in 1846, when Wajid Ali Shah was merely 24 years old. Although Wajid Ali explicitly states that she was a daughter of a *domni*, other sources indicate that Nawab Taz un-Nissa Begum Mashuq Mahal Saheba might have been the daughter of Ghulam Ali Khan.
75. *Zenana*: Refers to the secluded part of a traditional Muslim home, reserved exclusively for womenfolk. Derived from the Persian term, *zanānah*, from *zan* or woman.
76. *Khwajasara*: A transgender; often holding high position in the Nawabi court.
77. *Bawarchi*: Royal chef; cook.
78. *Phalsa*: Small purple edible berry, *Grewia asiatica.*
79. *Henna*: Myrtle. Essential oil from the plant can be used as a clear fresh scent.
80. The Twelve Imams are believed to be the spiritual and political successors to Prophet Mohammad according to the Shi'a faith.
81. *Sarod*: A stringed instrument used in Hindustani music, both for solo performances as well for accompaniment.
82. *Maulana*: Religious scholar in Islam.
83. *Talāq*: Divorce, according to Islamic tenets.
84. *Mut'ah*: Ancient Islamic practice uniting man and woman as husband and wife for a limited time, on mutual agreement.
85. *Mujra*: The singing and dancing of women, often prostitutes, in any cultural gathering.
86. *Kahar; kaharin:* Community of palanquin bearers. Female of this community.
87. *Habshi* / *Habshin*: Male / female of African (Abyssinian) origin.
88. *Lord Indra*: A Hindu deity; the dancing maidens of Lord Indra's court were celestial nymphs, considered to be extremely charming and beautiful, capable of wooing gods as well as

men with their talent of music, dance and captivating seductiveness. It is interesting that a Muslim ruler should refer to a divinity from the Hindu pantheon of Gods. But then, this was typical during Nawabi rule, which reached its zenith during Wajid Ali Shah's time.

89. *Haji:* Generally a person who has performed *Haj,* or pilgrimage to Mecca, although it can be an honorific title also in some cases.

90. *Ustād*: Maestro.

91. *Mujtahid:* One who is qualified to exercise *ijtihad* (reasoning / rationalising law on the basis of Islamic tenets) in the evaluation of Islamic law.

92. *Huzur-e-wala*: Eloquent address to an honourable personality.

93. *Musahib:* Courtier; friend and advisor.

94. *Raat ki Rani: Cestrum nocturnum* or night-blooming Jasmine - a small shrub with light green-yellow tubular flowers, which bloom at night with an intense fragrance but wither in day time.

95. *Farrash:* Cleaner, caretaker (primarily of carpets).

96. *Jumla*: False promises.

97. *Jān-é-Alam*: Literally "Spirit of the World." Wajid Ali Shah was affectionately referred to by this title, by members of his Court and admirers.

98. *Marsiya; Marsiya-khwani*: Elegy; reading of elegies (related to Muharram).

99. *Dhrupad raag*: A very old major vocal style associated with Hindustani classical music, with a single melodic line and no harmonic parts.

100. *Namaz*: Obligatory prayers prescribed in Islam, offered five times a day.

101. *Sadke jawaan:* I sacrifice myself to you.

102. *Houri:* A beautiful young woman, especially one of the virgin companions of the Faithful in Islamic belief.

103. *Hookah*: Hubble-bubble; water pipe.

104. An unsavoury incident by any standards, depicting the life and times of the young prince. His close contact and infatuation for women of low breeding, and his helplessness before their shenanigans would continue till late in life, giving an opportunity to his critics and to the British to label him as a debauch, all the while ignoring his immense talents, particularly in other literary fields.

105. *Chashm*: A spring, a fountain, spring, brook, source of running water.

106. *Gaj*: unit of land measurement; a square yard or 9 square feet. Hence *Chashm-e-Shireen* would have an area of 360 sq.ft. and the smaller *Chashm-e-Faiz* stream would be 135 - 90 sq.ft.

107. *Jogi* and *Jogan*; *Yogi and Yogini*: male and female Hindu ascetics. Those who withdraw from worldly affairs and devote their life in the service of God.

108. *Kamdhenu*: The divine bovine goddess in the Hindu pantheon, often called the "cow of plenty" who provides her owner whatever he desires and is often portrayed as a mother figure. The reader will note the constant references to Hindu divinity in this narrative - an apt illustration of the composite culture during the rule of the Awadh dynasty.

109. *Karaunda*: *Carissa carandas*, an attractive flowering shrub belonging to the *Apocynaceae* family. It produces berry-sized fruits, resembling cherries, that are commonly used as a condiment in Indian pickles and spices.

110. *Kamrak*: Also known as *Kamranga* or Star Fruit (Averrhoa carambola), a species of tree native to tropical SE Asia.

111. *Thandi Sadak*, literally Cold or Cool Road. This was behind the present day Chattar Manzil palace complex, on the river

side, but it lost its significance due to the change in the river's course, persistent flooding and construction of embankments to control the floods. Of late, there have been proposals of reviving it, but without the removal of the embankments, the possibility seems remote.

112. *Dupatta*: A long piece of cloth, draped around the head or body, as a sign of demureness.
113. *Khayal*: a musical form in Hindustani music having two parts that recur between expanding cycles of melodic and rhythmic improvisation.
114. *Saawan:* Second month of the rainy season in India. Commonly associated with feelings of romance and courtship, due to pleasant weather.
115. *Chote Saheb*: Junior master. Can denote "younger."
116. *Churidar*: Tight pyjama, with puckered bottoms and pleated at the top, worn both by males and females.
117. *Angrakha*: Literally "body-protector." A side open, long silk or cotton coat worn by men, usually covering the chest.
118. *Kotha:* Brothel; house of ill-repute.
119. *Risaldar*: Commander of the mounted troop.
120. *Ghazal*: Short poem in Urdu, consisting of couplets, often set to music, describing unrequited love (both spiritual as well as worldly) or the charms of intoxication.
121. *Raag Jhinjhoti:* A light and playful *raag*, apt for instrumental Hindustani classical music. A *raag* itself is a melodic framework, which has no parallel in western classical music.
122. *Thanedar*: In-charge of police station.
123. *Assalam va-'laikum*: Salutation meaning May Peace Be Upon You.
124. *Naib*: Deputy.
125. This firsthand account of *Sikandar Bagh* is no doubt informative. But it also reveals the tendency of the author to

use flowery epithets and exaggerate. The main building or dwelling of the *begum* in *Sikandar Bagh* was demolished after the events of 1857. But the gateway is still extant and so is the mosque. They are certainly not as grand and as magnificent as described in the text. If we learn from this example, the other flamboyant and often over-elaborate descriptions of people, events and places, including Nawabi gardens, become open to question about their genuineness.

126. *Rahas Leela* or *Raas Leela*: Denotes the "Dance of Divine Love" - a dance form narrating the love story of Lord Krishna (*a.k.a* Kanhaiya, Kanha, Madhusudan), Radha and the *gopis* (see below). It combines folk dance with the basic gestures of *kathak* story telling.

127. *Gopis*: Cowherd women who were devotees of Lord Krishna.

128. *Pooja:* Ritual performed by Hindus, (also Buddhists and Jains) to offer devotional homage and prayer to one or more deities, or to spiritually celebrate an auspicious event. Another shining example of the syncretism observed by Nawabi court at Lucknow.

129. *Kebab*: Meat patty, fried or grilled.

130. *Sheermal*: Sweet, aromatic flat bread.

131. *Naanbai*: One who prepares flat breads such as *roti, kulcha*, *sheermal* etc.

132. *Chausar; Chaupar*: Indian board game of great antiquity, a precursor of the modern Ludo. The board, in the shape of a cross, would be made of cloth or wool. *Cowries* (sea shells) would be used as tokens by the players.

133. *Chillum*: Funnel shaped water pipe, containing opium or *hashish.*

134. *Qawwali*: An energetic musical performance of Sufi Muslim poetry that aims to lead listeners to a state of religious ecstasy.

135. *Mazar*: Grave of a Muslim religious leader or saint.

136. *Surahi*: Earthen water pot.

137. Mohammad Shah "Rangila" (1702 - 1748), the 13th Mughal Emperor at Delhi was known for his patronage of the arts, including musical and cultural activities, including painting, earning him the sobriquet, "*Sadā Rangîla*" or "Ever Joyous."

138. Mohammed Adil Shah was the seventh ruler of Bijapur state in the Deccan. He ascended the throne at the age of 15. Besides territorial expansions, Bijapur attained peace and prosperity during Mohammed's reign. Cultural activities like poetry, painting and architecture also received a great impetus.

139. Tansen: Ramtanu Pandey (1500 - 1589), was a prominent exponent of Hindustani classical music, remembered for his epic Dhrupad compositions, creating several new ragas, as well as for writing two classic books on music. He was active in the court of Akbar, the Mughal Emperor.

140. Baiju: Baijnath Mishra a.k.a. *Baiju Bawra* was a great *Dhrupad* singer in the court of Akbar, the Mughal Emperor. He is famous for having defeated Tansen (see above) in a musical duel.

141. The Islamic calendar is also based on 12 months: *Muḥarram, Ṣafar, Rabīā al-Awwal, Rabīā al-Thānī, Jumādā al-Awwal, Jumādā al-Thānī, Rajab, Shabān, Ramaḍān or Ramzān* (the month of fasting), *Shawwāl, Dhū al-Qadah*, and *Dhū al-Ḥijjah*. Each month begins approximately at the time of the new moon.

142. *Dar-e-Daulat*: References to this crop up periodically in different accounts, and in various urban myths. Appears to have been a gateway in the *Kaiserbagh* palace complex, probably on the NE side, near *Sher Darwaza* or Neil's Gate. No longer extant, it must have been demolished during colonial rule, post 1857.

143. *Bandi: Bāndi* female slave; also loosely used for maid-servants.

144. Household; The term, used several times in the narrative can denote an actual domestic arrangement, or can refer to a harem in a polite and oblique way.
145. *Tola:* Traditional unit of weight in ancient India and south-east Asia. One *tola* = 11.66 gms.
146. *Sehri*: The pre-fasting meal consumed before dawn, during *Ramzān*.
147. Indicates the woeful status of the Nawabi court, when a Resident could ask a Crown Prince to meet him, and the latter obliged.
148. *Gulistan-e-Iram*: Part of the *Chota Chattar Manzil* seraglio, attributed to Nasir-ud-Din Haider. It was supposedly his library, and it was in the basement of this building that the king breathed his last. The building is still extant and has been recently restored by the UP Govt.
149. *Jannat Makān*: One who has an abode in the heavens = beautified. Wajid Ali Shah often referred to his late father, Amjad Ali Shah, in this manner.
150. *Mujtahid-ul*: Individual who is qualified to exercise *ijtihad* (reasoning / rationalising law on the basis of Islamic tenets) in the evaluation of Islamic law.
151. *Nazar*: Ceremonial gift presented in court to royalty / nobility.
152. *Baradari / Baradwari*: A building or pavilion with twelve entrances (or more), generally used for religious discourses.
153. Amin-ud-Daula: Credited for building the Amin-ud Daula market we see today in Lucknow.
154. *Doab*: Geographical tract in the Indo-Gangetic Plain having an area of about 23,360 square miles (60,500 square km), lying between the Ganges (Ganga) and Yamuna rivers.
155. *Naayak:* Corporal; military rank.
156. *Jaan-Nisaar*: Devoted; sacrificing one's life.
157. *Karnail:* Colonel; military rank.

158. The venerable Mallika Kishwar or Taj Ara Begum, *Khas Mahal* of Amjad Ali Shah and mother of Wajid Ali Shah, who died in France on January 23, 1858, after failing in her mission to petition Queen Victoria in London.

159. *Shah Manzil* formed part of the *Moti Mahal* palace complex, together with the *Mubarak Manzil.* These buildings were more popularly known as venues for viewing animal fights from across the river, than for holding marriage festivities.

160. Can a female member of a harem really refuse royal summons? The wonder of the royal persona seems misplaced here, since he was the one who had summoned the ladies in question in the first place.

161. The Narcissism is evident here, as observed earlier also.

162. Nasir-ud-Din Haider has been pilloried by western historians and writers for his unusual (= read undesirable) conduct as a ruler. However, this not-so-flattering reference to the king by another latter-day ruler of Awadh indicates that all was definitely not good with the unfortunate Nasir, who was reputed to have been poisoned to death, by his trusted maid servant, at the instigation of the British.

163. Not to be confused with Mughal Saheba, the daughter of Mohammad Ali Shah (third king of Awadh) whose elaborate *Imambara* and mosque are still extant (in a dilapidated condition) in *Wazir Bagh* area of old Lucknow.

164. *Daulat Khana-e-Asafi*: Palace complex at Lucknow on the banks of the river Gomti, built by Asaf-ud-Daula, fourth Nawab Wazir of Awadh (1775-1797).

165. *Panch Mahalla*: Five palace complex of Sheikh Abdur Rahim of Bijnaur, (who had been appointed as Subedar of Awadh by Emperor Akbar) which served as residences for himself and his sons. This would later form the nucleus for the *Macchi Bhavan*, the first citadel of the Nishapuri Nawabi dynasty at Lucknow. As the later rulers built their own palaces, the lesser

nobility continued to reside here, as well as in the *Daulat Khana* (see above).

166. Mohammad Ali Shah, the third king of Awadh, brother of Ghazi-ud-Din Haider, the first king. He was crowned as a successor to Ghazi-ud-Din in 1837 by the British. Credited for building the *Hussainabad* area in Lucknow and the monuments therein. Also credited for the *Al-Hur al-Riyahee* shrine outside the holy city of Karbala. With his ascension, the direct line of succession to the throne of Awadh changed, culminating in the rule of Wajid Ali Shah, the last king.

167. Badshah Begum, dowager queen of Ghazi-ud-Din Haider had been removed to Chunar fort by the British, soon after the ascension of Mohammad Ali Shah (see above).

168. Appears to have been the visit of Henry Hardinge, Governor General, during November 1847 (not to be confused with the later Charles Hardinge, who inaugurated the *Pakka Pul* or Hardinge Bridge in January, 1914. Charles Hardinge was the grandson of Henry Hardinge above).

169. *Chehlum* is a Shi'ite religious observance, held forty days after the martyrdom of Ali, the grandson of Mohammad. In this context, it is meant that the king would not accept that a perfidious woman had actually died, until mourning rites had been observed, forty days after her death.

170. Denoting sexual relations.

171. The Gregorian equivalent works out to be the years 1848 - 49. Wajid Ali Shah had been king for scarcely a year, when all this happened.

172. *Har* or हड़. A fruit used for its medicinal properties.

173. *Hakim:* A physician using *Unani* remedies in India and Islamic countries.

174. *Shaban* 15, also known as *Shab-e-Baraat*, a night for asking forgiveness.

175. *Badshah Manzil*: Part of *Kaiserbagh* palace complex; no longer extant now.
176. *Bismillah:* An invocation used by Muslims at the beginning of an auspicious task.
177. The constant, detailed references to Begum Hazrat Begum Saheba are very interesting, and certainly not very flattering.
178. *Imambara:* A congregation hall for Shi'a religious discourses, especially those associated with Muharram.
179. *Zu al-Hijjah*, is the twelfth and final month in the Islamic calendar. The date converts to November 5, 1849.

6

Epilogue: The King's Last Laugh

Mitra (2017), who was mentored by Meerza Kaukub, the great grandson of Birjis Qadr, while writing about the king's conduct in Lucknow and later, unwittingly stated, "*The ostentatious and vulgar Nawabi culture, which was visible in Wajid Ali Shah since his adolescence, has a different implication* (sic). *The heir-apparent of Awadh displayed a profligacy that worried his father and gave a free rein to scandalmongers*." We may never know if the late Kaukub Saheb subscribed to this disparaging view-point of Lucknow's Nawabi culture or of Wajid Ali Shah himself, but it is another example of the bundle of contradictions that Wajid Ali Shah was, during his lifetime, and even after his demise. Throughout history, he remained famous as a Nawab, although he was a ruling and then an exiled king. He was a devout Muslim, praying five times a day, a teetotaller, and yet was branded as a debauch and pervert. His writings and musical compositions were innovative and ahead of his times; nevertheless exponents such as Asadullah "Kaukab" Khan, a contemporary of Sharar were openly contemptuous of Wajid Ali's forays and innovations in music compositions. Sharar himself, who generally waxed eloquent about Lucknow, had written thus about the unfortunate Wajid Ali Shah, "*His character, therefore, appears to be one of the most dubious in all the records of history*."

After his coronation, for a period of two years, Wajid Ali had tried to zealously implement administrative reforms, which were

Fig. 13 : Courtesy *Ramayan-e-Khushtar*, Newal Kishore Press, Lucknow (1863).

compiled under his *Dastoor-e-Wajidi*, containing sixty six nos. dastoors (regulations). He had also attempted to upgrade his army. But his initiatives were actively discouraged by the British, who later accused him of misgovernance, oppression and misrule. This put an end to his youthful fervour as well as to his newly formed cavalry regiments having colourful names such as *Banka, Tircha* and infantry battalions named *Akhtari* and *Nadiri*. By his own admission he had *"arranged to have several wooden boxes glazed with silver, which would be carried by the royal guards accompanying the king. Any individual could place his petition or grievance in these boxes, which would be presented before me without delay. One day, some envelopes were recovered from these boxes. On examination, they contained unusual and strange accounts of Nawab Umrao Sahib, together with other mahals and begums. This system of petitioning was discontinued thereafter, because they began to cause me mental agony."* These petition boxes had been called *Mashgala-e-Nausherwani*. But his novel mechanism to address public grievances, first-hand, failed tragically.

Although highly secular-minded, the handling of certain communal disturbances during his rule exposed his inexperience as a young ruler and dependence on courtiers and officials, whose credentials and actions were questionable. The single most murky aspect at the fag end of his regime was the presentation of the Proclamation and Treaty of Annexation to the king by Outram, with the royal seal already in place. Who had affixed the royal seal, when the king had not actually signed the document? Possibly *Wazir* Ali Naqi Khan, his father-in-law and close confidante. In fact, the entire episode of Outram's taking over the administration of Awadh on February 7, 1856 after deposing Wajid Ali, continues to remain shrouded in controversy. On one hand, there are Outram's dispatches to Fort William and on the other hand, we have the writings of Kamal-ud-Din Haider and Najm-ul-Ghani. Also, it appears that Outram had been somewhat selective in his dispatches to Dalhousie. On the other hand, Kamal-ud-Din's narrative fails in chronology, as to whether the meeting between Outram and the king occurred on February 2 or 4, 1856. Another oversight on the part of Kamal-ud-Din was his claim that during Outram's meeting with Wajid Ali, the mother (Mallika Kishwar) and grandmother (Muqqadara Azma) of the king were also privy to the discussion from behind a *chilman* (screen). And Muqqadara Azma had even suggested that if Sikandar Hashmat was not a suitable replacement, then the candidature of Mustafa Ali could be considered. But a closer look at the historical timelines reveals that Muqqadara Azma had already died in October 1850.

Wajid Ali's interpersonal relations with his numerous queens and *mut'ah* wives and family were even more intriguing. His estrangement with Alam Ara Begum, his *Khas Mahal* has already been briefly described earlier. And yet, as per her status and loyalty, it was she who accompanied him to Calcutta. She had not stayed long with the king at *Chaulakhi Kothi* in *Kaiserbagh*, but preferred to stay independently at *Alambagh Kothi*, Lucknow. Similarly, at Calcutta, the deposed king had resided in the *Sultan Khana*, whereas Alam Ara Begum set up her own independent establishment at *Suroor Bagh*, near Garden Reach. While Wajid Ali's conflicts with the women of his establishment in Lucknow have been described by himself in *Ishqnama,* which covered only a brief period of his life, he remained a much married man in Calcutta also, with a sizable female population in *Metia Burz*. His love-hate relationship with Alam Ara Begum continued all throughout his lifetime. His relations with others, especially *mut'ah* wives were also full of quarrels. In 1878, he decided to dispense with twenty seven *mut'ah* wives, all at one go, having relieved forty - fifty nos. *mut'ah* wives earlier (Llewellyn-Jones, 2014). Some *mut'ah* wives preferred to return to Lucknow, while others quietly re-married. But what of the senior ones, like Mashuq Mahal? They too had to suffer ignominy at old age, petitioning the British for suitable allowances. Several of the children of the dispossessed wives too suffered a similar fate. His relations with Hamid Ali, son of Alam Ara Begum and heir apparent, (and later, a prince without a kingdom to inherit) as well as Farid-ud-Din Qadr, son of Mashuq Mahal, also remained ambivalent. Domestic squabbles were the norm, something which seemed unexpected from a man of Wajid Ali's talents and stature, but they did occur with alarming frequency. That British officials had to intervene frequently with their own Victorian values and supercilious attitude, only added further fuel to the fire. Also with time, Wajid Ali's menagerie had expanded exponentially, and so had the expenses on maintaining the animal collection. At one point of time, it seemed ironic that he had more affection for his animals and spent more time and money on his menagerie, than he did on his extended family of numerous wives and their offspring. The situation was slowly spiralling out of control.

Wajid Ali was a man who had even designed his own calendar, which he consulted for planning every major event in his life, including the fixing of auspicious occasions like marriages in the family. Prepared with the aid of master calligrapher, Syed Mohammed Mehdi Khan in Lucknow, the calendar remained in the king's possession till his last days in Calcutta. Yet it did not seem to have done him any good, as far as managing the events of his life was concerned.

There is no doubt that throughout his life, Wajid Ali suffered from bouts of illnesses, of varying idiopathic origins. This ranged from cardiac ailments to venereal disease and even anal fistula. It is beyond the scope of this book to discuss these. But even in death, the much maligned king seemed to have cheated his detractors. In as early as 1855, the British had become desperate to wrest control of Awadh, which was evident from the flurry of dispatches between the Lucknow Residency and Fort William, Calcutta. Under the tutelage of Lord Dalhousie, the intentions of the British crystallised from Sleeman onwards. Ironically, one of the concerns of our British benefactors was that the king could die anytime due to health issues, and as such, the kingdom of Awadh would be plunged into anarchy. On perusing the dispatches, it is obvious that although Wajid Ali Shah's son, Mirza Mohd. Hamid Ali was available as successor designate and heir apparent (*Wali Ahad*), the "death followed by anarchy" theory continued to be propounded, especially by Captain Hayes (later Military Secretary to Henry Lawrence). However, fate had other plans. Our favourite portly king outlived (by several decades), all his well-wishers, who had expressed so much concern about his imminent demise as follows: (1) WH Sleeman, died February 1856; (2) Captain Fletcher Hayes, shot dead in June 1857; (3) Lord Dalhousie, died December 1860; (4) James Outram, died March 1863; (5) Wajid Ali Shah, died September 1887.

Select Bibliography

Ahmad, EU, *Formation and End of a Mughal Provincial Civilization: A Socio-Economic and Cultural History of Awadh* (2008), Thesis for Ph.D, Aligarh Muslim University, Aligarh.

Akhtar, Wajid Ali Shah, *Pari Khana* (1965), Kitab Ghar, Rampur.

Akhtar, Wajid Ali Shah, *Pari Khana*, translated from Farsi by Shakeel Siddique (2017), Rajpal & Sons, New Delhi.

Ali, MH, *Observations on the Mussulmauns of India. Descriptive of their Manners, Customs, Habits and Religious Opinions made during Twelve Years Residence in Their Immediate Society* (1832), Humphrey Milford, London, UK.

Almeida, Hermione and Gilpin, GH, *Indian Renaissance: British Romantic Art and the Prospect of India* (2005), Ashgate Publishing Ltd., Aldershot, UK.

Anon, *Oude: Papers Relating To. Presented to both Houses of Parliament by Command of Her Majesty* (1856), Harrison & Sons, London.

Ansari, Tahir Hussain, "The Cultural and Literary Contribution of Nawab Wajid Ali Shah", *Int. J. English Language, Literature and Humanities*, Vol. II(III) (2014), pp. 181 – 189.

Awasthi, Preeti, *Awadh – Congenial Home for Nurturing Arts – In Historical Perspective of Painting and Music [1722 – 1856]* (2014), Thesis for Ph.D, University of Lucknow, Lucknow.

Azmi, AA, *The Annexation of Awadh and its Consequences* (1973), Thesis for Ph.D, Aligarh Muslim University, Aligarh.

Bahadur, Iqbal, *Parikhana* (1982), Sahitya Bhavan, Allahabad.

Barnett, Richard B, "Embattled Begams: Women as Power Brokers in Early Modern India" in Gavin RG Hambly (*ed.*) *Women in Medieval Islamic World: Power, Patronage and Piety* (1998), St. Martin's Press, New York, USA, pp. 521 - 536.

Basu, Prabir, *Nawab Wajid Ali Shah Ishqnama Athoba Parikhana-R Kissa* 1848 (1971), Lok Seva Shibir, Kolkata.

Bautze, JK, "Umrao Jan Ada: Her *carte-de-visite*" in Mevissen, GJR and Bannerji, A (*ed.*) *Prajnadhara: Essays on Asian Art, History, Epigraphy and Culture in Honour of Gouriswar Bhattacharya* (2009), Kaveri Books, New Delhi, pp. 137 - 154.

Bhatnagar, GD, *Awadh Under Wajid Ali Shah (*1968), Arun Press, Varanasi.

Bhatt, Ravi, *The Life and Times of The Nawabs of Lucknow* (2006), Rupa Publications, New Delhi.

Bird, RW, *The Spoliation of Oudh* (1857), Nassau Steam Press, Charing Cross, London, UK.

Brandreth, AM (*ed*). *Indian Engineering*, Vol. VIII (1879), Roorkee.

Casci, Simonetta, Casolari, Marzia and Vittorini, Simona, *Cultural and Political Identities in India* (2002), Casa, Milan, Italy.

Castro, G, *Wājid, Alî Shāh Plays Krishna's Stolen Flute: The Multiplicity of Voices in the King of Awadh's Dramatic Work* (2016), Thesis for Ph.D, University of Washington, Seattle, USA.

Chanda, S, Patnaik, A, and Chatterjee, S. C. (2021). "The Courtesan Project and the Tawa'ifs' Cultural Commons", *Int. J. of the Commons*, Vol. 15(1), (2021) pp. 195–205.

Chatterjee, Nandlal, *Glories of Uttar Pradesh* (1957), Publications Bureau, Information Department, UP, Lucknow.

Chaturvedi, KC, "Deposition of Wajid Ali Shah" *Proceedings of the Indian History Congress*, Vol. 23 (1960), pp. 62–68.

Choudhary, Manisha, "Domesticity, Religion and Politics: Exploring Life in Royal Palace of Awadh", *Int. J. Soc. Sc. Tomorrow*, Vol. 1(4) (2012), pp. 1-14.

Cole, JRI, *Roots of North Indian Shi'ism in Iran and Iraq - Religion and State in Awadh: 1722-1859 (1989),* University of California Press, Berkeley, USA.

Dalrymple, William, *White Mughals: Love and Betrayal in Eighteenth-Century India* (2004), Penguin, New Delhi.

Dehejia, HV, *Love Songs of Nawab Wajid Ali Shah* (2020), DK Print World, New Delhi.

Edwardes, Michael, *Orchid House: Splendours and Miseries of the Kingdom of Oudh, 1827 – 1857* (1960), Cassel, London, UK.

Fisher, Michael H, *A Clash of Cultures: Awadh, the British, and the Mughals (1987)*, Manohar Publishers & Distributors, New Delhi; *Idem., The Dynastic History of Lucknow*, http://www.academia.edu/4139086/The_Dynastic_History_of_Lucknow

Forrest, GW (*ed.*), *Selections from the Letters Dispatches and Other State Papers Preserved by The Military Department of The Government of India: 1857 – 58,* Vol. I (1893), Military Department Press, Calcutta.

Freitag, Sandra, "A Visual History of Three Lucknows", *J. South Asian Studies*, Vol. 37 (2014), pp. 431 – 453.

Freitag, Sandra, "Postscript. Interdisciplinary Dialogue and Lucknow's Cultural System", *S. Asia Multidisciplinary Academic Journal*, Vol. 11 (2015) pp. 1 - 16.

Gill, RS, *Indigenous Spectres, Subversive Lilas: Encounters Between Nawabi Authority, Colonialism and Popular Ritual In Lucknow* (2003), Thesis for MA, University of British Columbia, Vancouver, Canada

Graff, Violette (*ed.*), *Lucknow: Memories of A City* (1999), Oxford University Press, New Delhi.

Hansen, Kathryn, "The Beauties of Lucknow: An Urdu Photographic Album", *J. Urdu Studies*, (2020) pp. 141 - 176.

Hasan, Mushirul, *From Pluralism to Separatism: Qasbas in Colonial Awadh* (2012), Oxford University Press, New Delhi.

Hasnain, Nadeem, *The Other Lucknow* (2016), Vani Prakashan, New Delhi.

Howard, GES, *Courtesans in Colonial India: Representations of British Power through Understandings of Nautch Girls, Devadasis, Tawa'ifs. and Sex-Workers, c. 1750 - 1883* (2019), Thesis of MA (History), University of Guelph, Ontario, Canada.

Husain, Iqbal, "Awadh on the eve of 1857 - Evidence of the Urdu newspaper, *Tilism*", *Proceedings of the Indian History Congress*, Vol. 59 (1998) pp. 765–74.

Husain, Shaikh Tasadduq, *Begmat-i-Awadh* [Royal Women of Awadh] (1945), Kitab Ghar, Lucknow.

Keshani, Hussein, *Strangers, Lovers, and Kin: Gender Roles and Their Interplay with the Architecture of Awadh* (2003-2004), in *Studies on Architecture, History and Culture,* Aga Khan Program for

Islamic Architecture, Massachusetts Institute of Technology, Cambridge, USA.

Khan, AA, *Glimpses of The Arts of Awadh* (1989), State Museum, Lucknow.

Khan, Javed Ali. "*Sawanih Hayat Slatin Awadh* — An Introduction", *Proceedings of the Indian History Congress*, Vol.62 (2001) pp. 414–21.

Khatun, N, *Tawaifs and Islamicate Culture: Reading Bollywood's Muslim Women* (2020), in *Handbook of Research on Social and Cultural Dynamics in Indian Cinema*. IGI Global. https://doi.org/10.4018/978-1-7998-3511-0.ch008

Llewellyn-Jones, Rosie, *The Last King in India: Wajid Ali Shah* (2014), Random House India, Gurgaon.

Mahmud, Aslam, *Awadh Symphony: Notes on a Cultural Interlude* (2017), Rupa Publications, New Delhi.

Malleson, George Bruce, *The Indian Mutiny of 1857* (1891), Seeley & Co., London, UK.

McNeil, Adrian, "*Tawa'if*, Military Musicians and Shi'a Ideology in Pre-Rebellion Lucknow, South Asia", *J. of South Asian Studies*, Vol. 32(1) (2009) pp. 46-62.

Mitra, Sudipta, *Pearl By The River* (2017), Rupa Publications, New Delhi.

Mount, Ferdinand, *The Tears of The Rajas: Mutiny, Money and Marriage in India 1805 – 1905* (2015), Simon & Schuster, London.

Mukherjee, Rudrangshu, *Awadh in Revolt: 1857 – 1858* (2001), Permanent Black, Delhi.

Mukhopadhyay, Dilip, *Ajodhyar Nabab Wajid Ali Shah* (Bengali) (1984), Sankhya Prakasan, Kolkata.

Oldenburg, Veena Talwar, "Lifestyle as Resistance: The Case of the Courtesans of Lucknow, India", *Feminist Studies*, Vol. 16 (2) (1990) pp. 259–87.

Oldenburg, Veena Talwar, *Sham-e-Awadh: Writings on Lucknow* (2007), Penguin, New Delhi.

Pandey, RN, *Wajid Ali Shah aur Parikhana* (2013), Utkarsh Publishers, Kanpur.

Patel, A, "The Photographic Abums of Abbas Ali as Continuations of the Mughal Muraqqa Tradition", *Getty Research Journal*, Vol. 7 (2015) pp. 35 - 52.

Patel, A and Leonard, K (*eds.*), *Indo-Muslim Cultures in Transition* (2011), Brill Academic, Leiden, The Netherlands.

Petievich, Carla, *Assembly of Rivals: Delhi, Lucknow and the Urdu Ghazal* (1992), Manohar Publications, Delhi.

Pietrantonio, ND, "The Politics of Pleasure: Wajid Ali Shah and his Manuscript, *Ishqnama*", *Modern Asian Studies*, Vol. 55(5) (2020) pp. 1637 -1680.

Qaisar, Ahsan Jan, Verma, Som Prakash and Habib, Mohd. (*eds.*), *Art and Culture: Endeavours in Interpretation, Vol. 2* (1996), Abhinav, New Delhi.

Qidwai, Ikramuddin, "The Begams of Awadh and their Establishment", *Quarterly Journal of Pakistan Historical Society*, Vol. 38 (1990) pp. 309 – 328.

Qureshi, HA, *Sources on Awadh* (2004), New Royal Book Company, Lucknow.

Qureshi, HA, "A Note on The Harem of Shuja-ud-Daula", *UP Historical Review*, Vol. 1(1) (1982), pp. 63-64.

Qureshi, HA, *The Mughals, The English & The Rulers of Awadh from 1722 AD to 1856 AD. A Kaleidoscopic Study* (2003), New Royal Book Company, Lucknow.

Qureshi, MA, *Wajid Ali Shah's Theatrical Genius* (1987), Vanguard Press, New York.

Rizvi, SMH, Adeeb Irfan and Ayesha Irfan, "The Royal Stage of Lucknow", *Indian Literature,* Vol. 54 (5) pp. 170 - 186.

Rookmaaker, K, "The Royal Menagerie of the King of Oudh", *Back When, and Then*, Vol. II (1) (1997), pp. 10.

Sagar, Anand, *Wajid Ali Shah* (2019), National Paperbacks, New Delhi.

Sameen, Zoya, "Prostituting the *Tawa'if*: Nawabi Patronage and Colonial Regulation of Courtesans in Lucknow, 1847 - 1899", *Academia*, 11 June (2015) pp. 1 - 50.

Santha, K. Srinivasa, *Begums of Awadh* (1980), Bharati Prakashan, Varanasi.

Sarkar, PC, *Lucknow: Buildings, Begums and The British* (2015), Kalpaz, New Delhi.

Sarkar, PC, *Lucknow - Ode To A City* (2021), Kalpaz, New Delhi.

Sarwari, Tehsin, *Parikhana* (1965), Delhi Printing Press, Rampur.

Sharar, Abdul Halim, *Lucknow: The Last Phase of an Oriental Culture* (1989), translated by Harcourt, ES and Hussain, Fakhir, Oxford University Press, New Delhi.

Sharma, AK, *Begum Hazrat Mahal* (2015), Gyan, New Delhi.

Sinh, Ranbir, *Wajid Ali Shah - The Tragic King* (2002), Publication Scheme, Jaipur.

Singh, Parul, "Staging Power: Visual Strategies of Kingship in the Windsor Castle *Ishqnama* Illustrated Manuscript", *J. British Institute of Persian Studies*, Vol. 59 (2021) pp. 308 - 321.

Singh, Shalini, *Cultural Tourism In The Awadh Region with Special Reference to Lucknow* (1992), Thesis for Ph.D, University of North Bengal, Darjeeling.

Singh, SN, *The Kingdom of Awadh: Its History, Polity and Administration* (2003), Mittal, New Delhi.

Singh, VP, "From *Tawaif* to Nautch Girl: The Transition of the Lucknow Courtesan", *South Asian Review*, Vol. 35(2) (2014) pp. 177-194.

Sleeman, William H, *A Journey Through the Kingdom of Oudh in 1849 – 185,* Vol. 1 & 2 (1858), Richard Bentley, London, UK.

Sleeman, William H, *Rambles and Recollections of an Indian Official* (1915), Oxford University Press, London, UK.

Sprenger, A, *A Catalogue of the Arabic, Persian and Hindustani Manuscripts of the Libraries of the King of Oudh*, Vol. I (1854), Baptist Mission Press, Calcutta.

Srivastava, AL, *Shuja-ud-Daulah, Vol. I: 1754 – 1765* (1961), SL Agarwala, Agra.

Srivastava, AL, *Shuja-ud-Daulah, Vol. II: 1765 – 1775* (1945), Minerva, Lahore.

Srivastava, AL, *The First Two Nawabs of Awadh* (1954), SL Agarwala, Agra.

Susewind, R and Taylor, CB, "Introduction. Islamicate Lucknow Today: Historical Legacy and Urban Aspirations", *S. Asia Multidisciplinary Academic Journal*, Vol. 11 (2015) pp. 1 – 23.

Wali, Abdul, *Sorrows of Akhtar: An Autobiographical Account of the Deposition and Imprisonment of the Sultan-e-Alam Wajid Ali Shah, the Last King of Oudh* (1926), Baptist Mission Press, Calcutta.

Walker, M., (2010). "Revival and Reinvention in India's Kathak Dance", *MUSICultures*, Vol. 37 (2010) pp. 171–184.

Williams, RD, *Hindustani Music Between Awadh and Bengal, c. 1758 - 1905* (2014), Thesis for Ph.D, King's College, London, UK.

Annexure - I

List of Books Written by Wajid Ali Shah

(Persian, Urdu and Hindustani Languages)

The actual number of books written by Wajid Ali Shah could never be listed unequivocally till date. Multiplicity of languages, as also translations and versions of the same book under different / alternative names have resulted in this confusion. It is also surmised that many of his writings might have got lost the events of 1857 at Lucknow and also after his demise in Calcutta, with the British being in a hurry to dispose off his assets. Hence, the alphabetical list presented below is at best indicative and may also contain duplicate entries due to reasons stated above; it does not claim to be authoritative or exhaustive. At best, it reflects the immense genius of a royal prince / king, who was maligned and deposed, and yet whose abundance of talents, particularly in the literary and cultural field, remained unsurpassed till his last days.

1. *Afah-e-Suinyah*
2. *Afsana-e-Ishq*
3. *Bahar-e-Ulfat*
4. *Bani*
5. *Chanchal Nazanin*
6. *Daftar-e-Ghum-o-Bahr-e-Aalam*
7. *Dar Fan-e-Mausiqi*
8. *Darya-e-T'ashuq*
9. *Dastoor-e-Wajidi*
10. *Diwan Ghazaliyat*
11. *Diwan-e-Akhtar*
12. *Diwan-e-Mubarak*
13. *Dulhan*
14. *Guldastah-e-Ashiqan*
15. *Habat-e-Haidari*
16. *Husn-e-Akhtar*
17. *Iman*
18. *Imran*
19. *Intikhab-e-Wajid Ali Shah Akhtar*

20. *Irshad-e-Khaqani*
21. *Ishqnama / Parikhana*
22. *Jawab-e-Bluebook*
23. *Jild Marasi*
24. *Juhar-e-Uruz*
25. *Khitabat-e-Mahallat*
26. *Kuliyat-e-Akhtari*
27. *Mahiyat-ul-Ghina*
28. *Malaz-ul-Kalmat*
29. *Masnavi Dar Halat-e-Gunna Tawaif*
30. *Masnavi-e-Gunn*
31. *Mazhabi Marsia*
32. *Mubasah Bayn Al-nafs Va'al-'aql*
33. *Mulaz-ul-Kalamat*
34. *Mulk-e-Akhtari* or *Akhtar-e-Mulk*
35. *Musummi-Ba-Banni*
36. *Naat*
37. *Najo*
38. *Nami-e-Namwar*
39. *Nasha-e-Akhtari*
40. *Nazm-e-Namwar*
41. *Nazo* (Hindustani)
42. *Noha*
43. *Qamar-e-Mazmun*
44. *Qanun-e-Akhtari*
45. *Qasaid-ul-Mubarak*
46. *Radha Kanhaiya Ka Qissah*
47. *Risala-e-Iman*
48. *Risala-e-Mausiqui*
49. *Riyaz-ul-Quloob*
50. *Riya-ul-Uqba*
51. *Sabat-ul-Quloob*
52. *Sahifa-e-Sultani*
53. *Sarma-e-Imaan*
54. *Saut-ul-Mubarak*
55. *Shivn-e-Faiz*
56. *Shua-e-Faiz*
57. *Sukhan-e-Ashraf*
58. *Tarikh-e-Badr*
59. *Tarikh-e-Bahar*
60. *Tarikh-e-Firaq*
61. *Tarikh-e-Ghazala*
62. *Tarikh-e-Jamshedi*
63. *Tarikh-e-Mozahib*
64. *Tarikh-e-Mumtaz*
65. *Tarikh-e-Noor*
66. *Taushi'a-e-Akhtar*

Annexure - II

Listing of Daroga Abbas Ali's Album, *The Beauties of Lucknow* in Digital Collection of New York Public Library

- Feerozah dancing girl of the Oudh Court of Lucknow, Pl. 1
- Gowhur dancing girl of the Oudh Court of Lucknow, Pl. 2
- Mushtari dancing girl of the Oudh Court of Lucknow, Pl. 3
- Zohrah dancing girl of the Oudh Court of Lucknow Pl. 4
- Pl. 5 - Missing
- Ameer Jan, Biba Wali dancing girl of the Oudh Court of Lucknow, Pl. 6
- Husso Jan dancing girl of the Oudh Court of Lucknow, Pl. 7
- Ameer Jan, Biba Wali dancing girl of the Oudh Court of Lucknow, Pl. 8
- Nazeer of Chundurbhga. Dancing girl of the Oudh Court of Lucknow, Pl. 9
- Oomraujan dancing girl of the Oudh Court of Lucknow, Pl. 11
- Abadee dancing girl of the Oudh Court of Lucknow, Pl. 12
- Hosensee dancing girl of the Oudh Court of Lucknow, Pl. 13
- Juddan dancing girl of the Oudh Court of Lucknow, Pl. 14
- Soondur dancing girl of the Oudh Court of Lucknow, Pl. 15
- Lall-Purree of the Indur Subha. Dancing girl of the Oudh Court of Lucknow, Pl. 16
- Pookhraj-Purree of the Indur Subha. Dancing girl of the Oudh Court of Lucknow, Pl. 17

- Subuz-Purree of the Indur Subha. Dancing girl of the Oudh Court of Lucknow, Pl. 18
- Rajah Indur of the Indur Subha with Giants ("Deoo"). At the Oudh Court of Lucknow, Pl. 19
- Ubbasee Domnee. Dancing girls and musicians of the Oudh Court of Lucknow, Pl. 20
- Ladlee dancing girl from the Oudh Court of Lucknow, Pl. 22
- Gummoon dancing girl from the Oudh Court of Lucknow, Pl. 23
- Hydur Jan dancing girl from the Oudh Court of Lucknow, Pl. 24

Index

C

D

I

J

N

T